MW00806189

WHO KILLED...?
PITTSBURGH, PA

ROOFTOP
publishing

Rooftop Publishing™
1663 Liberty Drive, Suite 200
Bloomington, IN 47403
Phone: 1-800-839-8640

This book is a work of non-fiction. Unless otherwise noted, the author and the publisher make no explicit guarantees as to the accuracy of the information contained in this book and in some cases, names of people and places have been altered to protect their privacy.

©2007 Rooftop Publishing. All rights reserved

No part of this book may be reproduced, stored in a retrieval system, or transmitted by any means without the written permission of the author.

First published by Rooftop Publishing 09/28/2007

Publisher: Kevin King
Senior Editor: Lesley Bolton
Cover Design: Lauren Allen
Book Design: Jessica Sheese
Production Manager: Aaron Schultz
Senior Publicist: Shannon White

ISBN: 978-1-60008-040-1 (sc)

Library of Congress Control Number: 2007931129

"Who Killed ...?" is a trademark of Rooftop Publishing

Printed in the United States of America
Bloomington, Indiana

This book is printed on acid-free paper.

A Tribute to Russell Elliott

The "Who Killed ...?" series is a tribute to the memory of Russell Elliott of Bloomington, IN, who was murdered on April 7, 2004, and to all unsolved murder victims across our country who deserve to be recognized and their killers brought to justice. Should you have information about the Russell Elliott case, please contact Detective B.W. Smith at 317-367-1051.

INTRODUCTION

Since the days of Cain and Abel, people have murdered one another for various reasons. FBI statistics show that of the 16,137 murders across the country in 2004, only 64 percent were solved, and out of that percentage, 70.2 percent have been committed by an acquaintance of the deceased. We will be examining some of the remaining percent of those untimely deaths that are to this date unsolved. Yes, it is a small percentage; nonetheless, it is a statistic that stands out as being the most intriguing number of murders that are committed. These are the most gruesome or heartbreaking of cases that society, families, and law enforcement are unable to forget.

As you read these cold-blooded cases, pay close attention to the facts outlined and other details being provided. We are not claiming to be able to solve any of these crimes; our only intent is to bring these murders back into the public's eye. With the passing of time, hopefully someone will come forward now with information helpful to close these cases and bring the guilty to justice. Police agencies along with the victims' families are asking for your help in solving these crimes. Investigating officers' names and/or phone numbers are included at the closing of each story, and we urge you to call with any information that could be helpful in the arrest and conviction of the killers. You will also find our E-mail address if you would rather contact us directly, and the information will be passed along to the proper authorities.

This second book in our "Who Killed …?" series takes place in Pittsburgh and its surrounding areas. The riverfront portal city is easily identified as the home of the Pittsburgh Pirates and Steelers, but these sports franchises only represent a small part of the city's economic development over the past twenty years. In May 2007, Pittsburgh was once again named "most livable city" by *Places Rated Almanac*—recognition Pittsburgh hasn't been able to enjoy since 1985, when current mayor Luke Ravenstahl was only five years old. During those years, the murder rate was 2.1 times the national average, according to FBI statistics. It wasn't until 2006 that Pittsburgh began to see a decline in its citizens being brutally killed. Another statistic Ravenstahl and mayors in surrounding cities are not pleased with is a high rate of those same murders going unsolved. It's here that we will begin to unfold the truth, fact, and fiction of this region's killers and unsolved murders by asking the question, "Who killed …?"

Contents

1. Who Killed Edward "Mr. Jimmy" Loggins?............................1
2. Who Is "The Shotgun Killer"?..5
3. Who Killed 13-year-old Barbara Ann Barnes?....................21
4. Who Killed John Yelenic the Day Before His Divorce?......29
5. Who Killed Catherine Corkery?...37
6. Who Is the Washington County Strangler?.........................45
7. Who Killed Jamie Lynn Stickle?...55
8. Who Killed Raymond Marzoch?...61
9. Who Killed Sandra Baker?..67
10. Who Killed 16-year-old Raquel Tilisha Carter?.................75
11. Who Killed My Sons?..79
12. Who Killed Robert Kart?...83
13. Who Killed Jane Doe and Her Unborn Child?..................89
14. Who Killed My Mother?..93
15. Who Wrote to Police Confessing to Murder?....................97
16. Who's Killing Under Protection of The Code?................105
17. Who Killed the Police Informant?....................................115
18. Who Killed Chief of Police Gregory Adams?...................139
19. Who Killed Michael and Mary Brincko?..........................145
20. Who Killed Bonnie Dryfuse and Her Children?..............149
21. Other Unsolved Murder Cases Throughout Pennsylvania 155

Who Killed Edward "Mr. Jimmy" Loggins?

Edward Loggins, pictured to the left, finally accepted his well-deserved retirement and gold watch in 2002 after working for USX Corporation for forty-one years. Edward was most remembered as a receptionist and bartender for the sixty-first-floor executive offices of the U.S. Steel Tower. Before his career with USX, Edward was said to have once worked as a military police officer during World War II in Washington DC and helped guard then-president Truman.

Known to everyone as "Mr. Jimmy," Edward soon found he missed his work and countless friends he'd made over the years. Unknown to most people who only saw him in their own day-to-day lives, "Mr. Jimmy" was a world of knowledge and life experiences that would touch everyone he came in contact with. Since retiring, Edward could not just sit at home and not be actively doing something. "He'd get on a bus and just ride, every day, seven days a week, no particular spot," said eighty-one-year-old wife Jacqueline, who met Edward in 1947 when a cousin introduced them. "As long as he was talking to people, he was happy."

That was just the way he was, a relative remembers. He couldn't just sit home and watch the soap operas and game shows. So, most days he would get up in the morning and make his way to the bus stop, using a walker to steady himself, then make the routine ride downtown to McDonald's, where the employees sometimes had his tray with a Happy Meal and a Coke waiting for him. Occasionally they didn't even charge him, saying, "Mr. Jimmy, it's on us."

He often visited the U.S. Steel Tower to call on old friends and withdraw some money at the credit union, but never more than $25, which would last him a week. For the most part, he just rode the buses with no real destination, getting off at the end of the line and taking another bus back.

On April 19, 2007, "Mr. Jimmy" had a specific destination in mind. After making his normal visit to the McDonald's on Smithfield Street at 7:45 a.m., he re-boarded a bus and was last seen on transit authority videotape on a bus to the Century III Mall in West Mifflin that arrived there at about 11 in the morning. Surveillance camera images from inside the bus show Edward aboard with his walker, dressed in a trench coat and slacks. He was found dead at 12:43 p.m. on the railroad tracks on the Mon-Line section of Norfolk and Southern railroad in Baldwin borough. He had been shot once in the head, and his pockets had been turned inside out. Police suspect he may have accepted a ride from someone who then robbed and killed him in Baldwin.

The motive is believed to be robbery, and whoever killed Edward stole his walker, personal phone book, cash, and health card—leaving behind the gold watch only because they would not be able to fence it with Mr. Loggins' name inscribed inside. Public outcry to such a brutal act against an eighty-six-year-old citizen quickly spread throughout the entire state. Crime Stoppers immediately offered a reward of up to $1,000 for information leading to the arrest and prosecution of the killer. His family soon after started a fundraiser in hopes of increasing the reward amount to entice someone to come forward and solve his murder.

People began speaking out publicly and in the media about how they remembered "Mr. Jimmy" and the impact he made on their lives. "I am a Port Authority driver who had the pleasure of taking Mr. Loggins on many of his Saturday excursions," wrote Barbara Schrader. "He always tried to teach me new words in another language. I usually forgot the words, but I will never forget this kind and gentle man who touched so many lives."

His daughter, Gloria Mott, said, "It boggles my mind. It's such a mystery who would do that to such a man who lived his life as an example. He never met a stranger. He would get on the bus and start talking to someone who maybe didn't want to talk at first, someone who was grumpy and going to work, and by the end of the ride they would be happy and smiling."

Others remembered he was the kind of old-fashioned gentleman who shined his shoes every day, held a door open for a lady, and always wore a white shirt even while painting his house or trimming his hedges. Fellow bus riders who barely knew him took the time to sign his online obituary guestbook.

"I too was yet another bus rider that was touched by Mr. Jimmy," wrote one person. "I didn't know his name, but when I saw him I always had to smile. I often wondered about his life, as he was such a charming and charismatic person. When I heard the news, I actually felt a tug at my heart and a tear in my eye for the loss of his life. Mr. Loggins seemed to have such an effect on people, and will truly be missed."

Police still ask for your help with this unsolved murder of Edward Loggins. They have said not to discount the relevance of any information you may know. Your piece of information may have a significant impact on the investigation when viewed in the context of what they already know. For further information, call Pittsburgh police at (412) 255-8477, or you can E-mail whokilled@rooftoppublishing.com, and we will pass along this information.

Research and development for this story was made possible by the assistance of the Pittsburgh Public Library, *Pittsburgh Post* and *Tribune-Review* newspapers, Pittsburgh police, and the friends and family of "Mr. Jimmy."

Who Is "The Shotgun Killer"?

Born on August 8, 1941, in Aliquippa, Pennsylvania, Edward Arthur Surratt, pictured to the left, was the only child born to Arthur Edward and Anna Mae Surratt. He was raised in the section of town commonly known as "the hill," and educated in Aliquippa's schools. His parents were respected Georgia transplants to the hill, which was at that time a bustling area full of social clubs and churches. His father came to Pennsylvania sometime in the 1930s and worked as a butler, as a farmer, and at J&L Steel Corporation in Aliquippa. He also operated his own successful refuse collection company. Folks on the hill knew him and his wife as hard workers and doting parents. Anna Mae liked to dress her son well.

Surratt's boyhood schoolmate remembered that he and Surratt were bumped through fifth and sixth grades in the same year. In those days at Jones Elementary School, teachers would "double-promote" kids based on intelligence. Surratt was very outgoing, always laughing and telling jokes, the friend said. He had a happy-go-lucky demeanor. Eddie Surratt never had a nasty word to say, and his parents went to school functions. Something changed Surratt in Vietnam, many thought. But his trouble predated the war. Aliquippa police arrested Surratt while he was in high school for loitering and prowling on nights in 1959 and 1960. During the second incident, Surratt broke the arresting officer's nose. He was convicted of the loitering charge and assault on a police officer and spent fourteen months in state prison at Camp Hill. Also in 1960, an Aliquippa woman filed charges of "fornication and bastardy" against Surratt for conceiving an illegitimate child with her daughter the year before. Surratt was ordered to pay $8.50 a week to support the child, who later came to live with Surratt's parents.

Although he was said to be a good student early on, by high school Surratt had problems. He eventually graduated in 1960 with a D+ average, 186 out of a class of 298. In 1963, Surratt's parents told the *Times* newspaper their son had made the dean's list at Youngstown State University, where he was a freshman studying pre-med. The college stint lasted only that year. Police and military records show that in March 1964 he underwent U.S. Army basic combat training at Fort Dix, New Jersey. In June, he took the basic army chaplain course and served as an assistant chaplain. Sometime in 1964, the same records show Surratt paid a fine for assaulting a man with a pipe. And by April 1965, he was reduced in rank for going AWOL.

The next time Edward Surratt appeared in the newspaper was June 1965, and his grinning, good-looking face sported a helmet and chinstrap. He had completed airborne training. During the same year, he was arrested for reckless driving, leaving the scene of an accident, driving without a license, and carrying an unregistered firearm. He was fined $200. In another case, Surratt faced a charge of loitering or prowling at night. The case was dismissed for lack of evidence. Both happened during his stay in the army.

In June 1965, his father died of lung cancer. Two months later, Surratt got an honorable "hardship" discharge and was released to the U.S. Army Reserve. He returned to Aliquippa to run his father's garbage business until it folded in 1966. His obligation to the Army Reserve ran out on October 3, 1966. He enlisted in the U.S. Marine Corps the next day. His mom bragged to friends that Eddie liked the "rough stuff." He arrived in Vietnam in the spring of 1967 in an amphibious tractor battalion team. These soldiers most often were seen jumping from the beds of landing craft into the surf and the heat of battle. Surratt participated in eleven combat expeditions during two tours of duty, according to military records.

In 1967, Surratt took part in search-and-destroy missions in the Da Nang rocket belt that resulted in the destruction of 6,000 communist bunkers, tunnels, and shelters, according to military records. Surratt told an investigator he was in the Tet Offensive in 1968, arguably the defining year of the Vietnam War. By the time he was transferred to Subic Bay in the Philippines in September for duties as a guard and later a platoon sergeant, Surratt had suffered a shrapnel wound to his chest and a ruptured eardrum.

Surratt also told the investigator he had been in a foxhole when Viet Cong in loincloths threw in an explosive, blowing him and his partner out of the hole. Surratt said he was temporarily blinded and deaf. The first thing he saw was his partner standing without an arm. Surratt played dead as their position was overrun, and the secondary force killed off the enemy. He went back into battle from July 1970 until he was discharged in late September 1970. He came home with several medals, most of them common service medals, except for the Republic of Vietnam Cross of Gallantry with palm and frame, and a Purple Heart.

Surratt returned from Vietnam to North Carolina. He married Offia, a North Carolina native, in October 1970 and began a long pattern of short stints with a number of trucking companies. On some of his job applications he claimed attendance at a truck driving school and a plumbing school in North Carolina. In 1973, while he still lived in North Carolina, Virginia Beach (Virginia) police arrested Surratt for sodomy, abduction, and enticement charges involving a thirteen-year-old boy. He was found guilty of all charges except abduction in March 1974 and spent three years in prison. Details of the crime are not available. In January 1977, Surratt returned to Aliquippa. That's when the local killing started.

September 20, 1977

That night, Linda Hamilton, pictured to the left with her children, slept through a thunderstorm. The couple's children, five-year-old Melynda and three-year-old Christopher, had crawled into bed at 9 p.m. David Hamilton watched late-night TV in the living room in his T-shirt and underwear. Next-door neighbors heard what sounded like strong, rapid strokes of a hammer at 12:45 a.m. Seconds before, a knock had sounded on the Hamiltons' kitchen door. David answered. Three rounds from a .38-caliber handgun hit him in the back of his head and each of his shoulders as he turned to run. He collapsed and died in the entryway. The children found David, pictured below, there in the morning and ran to the neighbors.

They never saw their mother again. Police found the couple's car near the entrance of a closed strip mine in view of the truck stop where Linda worked. Found were prints of a man's boots and Linda's bare feet sometimes walking and sometimes dragging as if she had been  pulled from the driver's side. Later, neighbors in the modest blue-collar area remembered seeing a black man walking down the road from the direction of the truck stop. A bicycle found in the Hamiltons' yard was stolen from the garage of a house along that trek. In between, people discovered flowerpots toppled as though someone had tried to peer through their windows.

Initially, the Mahoning County Sheriff's Department suspected Linda of killing her husband. It issued a fugitive warrant, which prompted a federal warrant for her arrest, and kept it active for several years after her disappearance. Beaver Township Ohio Police Chief Carl Frost always thought it was clear that Linda was abducted. But when Frank Ziegler, twenty-eight, a driver for Taylor Milk Company in Ambridge, turned up shot to death a week later, the Mahoning sheriff believed Linda Hamilton was the killer.

September 27, 1977

Ziegler was bound for his farm from Taylor's loading dock in Ambridge. Police don't know what led him to pull off the road that night. Ziegler, of Kittanning, was shot once in the head in his milk tanker truck on Warrendale Bayne Road in Marshall Township, Allegheny County. The community borders Economy. The call initially came in as a suicide, but police found no gun at the scene. They found the contents of Ziegler's wallet strewn inside the cab and on the road's berm. Four hundred dollars was missing. Ballistics tests showed the same .38-caliber gun that had killed David Hamilton killed Ziegler. Allegheny County police didn't make the connection the Mahoning sheriff was sure of. A killer was loose, but Allegheny officials didn't think it was Linda Hamilton. Three days later, Joseph and Katherine Weinman turned up dead in their Marshall Township home.

September 30, 1977

The Weinmans' one-story house in Marshall was in a rural setting within easy walking distance of the Pennsylvania Turnpike. Joe, thirty, became a paraplegic when he was machine-gunned in the back in Vietnam. He got around either on a gurney or a wheelchair. Kathy, twenty-eight, cared for him and their two young boys, five-year-old Joe Jr. and two-year-old Kenny. That night, the children slept as Joe lay on his stomach on the gurney so Kathy could dress an ugly half-dollar-sized bedsore on his buttock. Joe, nude, was outside the bathroom door as Kathy nursed him when the killer confronted them. Police never found the weapon he used but think the killer took a five-pound sledgehammer discovered to be missing from the garage.

He slammed the weapon into Joe's head then chased Kathy around the home, beating her, stripping her of her clothes, and raping her. In the meantime, Joe regained consciousness. He wheeled himself down the hall. In a closet was a shotgun. It was inoperable, but he thought it possibly would be a deterrent, a bluff. The killer caught him at the open closet door before he could reach the gun and hit him from behind, caving in his skull. Kathy ran. She made it to the gravel drive before the killer caught her. He killed her with at least eleven stab wounds to her face and chest area and cut her throat with one of her steak knives taken from the drain bin on the kitchen sink.

Her little boys, who hid all night in fear under a bed, found her there face up in the morning. Hairs from her killer were clutched in her hand; her right index finger was broken from the struggle. Joe Jr. ran to a neighbor's house for help. The boy told officers he saw the killer from his room. He was a "bank robber," the boy said. He wore a red bandana around the lower half of his face. Again, police had little to go on. From the hair roots they determined the killer was probably black and had type A-positive blood. From prints they learned he wore size 10 shoes. But those were their only clues.

October 22, 1977

John Feeny, seventeen, pictured to the left, of Coraopolis was shot to death in his parents' van while parking with his date, Ranee Gregor, fifteen, pictured to the left, of Robinson Township, along a lonely lovers' lane in Findlay Township. No trace of Ranee, a pretty junior at Montour High School just days from her sweet sixteenth, was ever found.

November 10, 1977

The killer came in the morning for sixty-three-year-old John Davis and his wife, Mary. It was John's birthday. The couple rose and made coffee in the kitchen of their isolated single-story structure about one hundred yards from the road. Across the road, patchy woods stretched to behind the same truck stop in Beaver Township where Linda Hamilton had worked. The killer came to the back door. John took a blast from a 12-gauge shotgun in the eye at close range. Mary probably drew her last breath in their bedroom, where the killer stripped her, shot her in the chest, and left her spread-eagled. At some point, he also shot their dog in the basement.

The killer then took a gas can from the Davises' garage, doused the couple, and set them on fire. Passing motorists reported the blaze late that afternoon. Portions of the home were destroyed. The bodies of the Davises were intact but charred. Any evidence of the killer was destroyed.

November 20, 1977

The relatively calm Beaver County residents felt their world was shattered. That morning, seven-year-old Billy Adams woke in his bed in the family's secluded mobile home off Route 51 in Fallston. His little four-year-old sister, Wendy Jo, woke shortly after him. They found their father, William Adams Jr., thirty-one, dead on his bedroom floor. He was nude and lying on his back, his chest mangled from the close-range blast of a 12-gauge shotgun. Their mom, Nancy, was gone. No signs of a struggle disrupted the place. Despite some valuable possessions in the home, family members didn't notice anything missing. Nancy's purse and keys were still inside. Police could find no trace of the intruder. Searchers covered the surrounding woods and area for miles and found nothing. Nancy Adams' remains wouldn't be found until eight years later, in nearby Brady's Run Park.

December 3, 1977

Police officers responded to a call at a one-story ranch home on Shafer Road in Moon Township. There they found two shocked girls, nine-year-old Kelli and her four-year-old sister Karri, daughters of Richard and Donna Hyde. Richard,

thirty-four, the well-liked principal of Fern Hollow Elementary School in Moon, lay dead face down on the kitchen floor. A blast from a 12-gauge shotgun had mangled his chest. His thirty-four-year-old wife, Donna, pictured to the left, who had had a beautician's business in their basement, was missing. Police later found her partially clad body beneath a pine tree face up. Something like a blackjack had been used to strike her head repeatedly, leaving several cuts. But Donna had not been raped. Police thought barking dogs at a nearby home had frightened off her attacker. She died from the beating and exposure to the bitter cold. Police discovered that the shell casing found at the end of the hallway in the Hydes' home matched the casing found in the Adams' home.

December 31, 1977

A couple in Breezewood, off the Pennsylvania Turnpike in Bedford County, saw the killer coming, but they didn't realize it and did nothing to stop him. The elderly couple was preparing to celebrate New Year's when the husband noticed a black man looking in his window. He didn't bother to notify the police, and the peeper went away. The killer then went to another ranch-style home nearby. There he knocked on the kitchen door. Guy Mills, sixty-four, had been watching TV and answered. The killer shot him at point-blank range. He then walked into the living room and shot sixty-four-year-old Donna Mills in her bedclothes. Their grown grandson who lived with them found both bodies when he returned home.

Police had also found the body of Joel Drueger, thirty-six, of Altoona. He was in his car four miles away at a rest stop on Interstate 70. He was killed with the same shotgun used on the

Mills. Police were perplexed by the killings until people came forward to report they'd seen a car that night at an abandoned gas station. The car, a Buick Electra, was parked a short distance downhill from the Mills' home. The people who spotted it sandwiched between two semis thought it curious enough to jot down the license plate number. A check produced the owner's name and address: Edward Surratt of Aliquippa.

When state police contacted officers in Beaver County about Surratt, pieces started to fall together. The Mills had been killed in much the same way as the others in this area. Though Donna Mills wasn't beaten or raped, other similarities were enough to interest police. And although Drueger's death didn't fit the pattern, it was similar to the death of Ziegler, the Taylor Milk truck driver killed in Allegheny County. Ziegler's and Drueger's cases also were directly connected to the other deaths because the guns used to kill them were used to kill victims who did fit the pattern.

Police finally had a suspect.

Surratt, they learned, was a long-distance truck driver and former garbage hauler. Suddenly it made sense that all the murder sites were near major routes, truck stops, and garbage dumps. Feeny and Gregor were parking near a garbage dump, a place Surratt knew. The Hydes lived near another garbage dump. The rest lived near major trucking routes.

Police already had used a psychologist to examine information from crime scenes and had come up with a personality profile. In his report, the psychologist surmised the killer was a combat veteran, most likely from the Vietnam War. He also figured the killer was symbolically killing his mother and father; was of above-average intelligence, white, and divorced or separated; had been betrayed by a woman; was a loner; and worked in a job involving driving. The psychologist also theorized the killer suffered from paranoid schizophrenia that he was able to disguise. As police began an intensive background study of Edward Surratt, they found many of the psychologist's summations to be compatible. The most obvious discrepancy was that Surratt was black. To this day, black serial killers are rare. Most are white, which perhaps led the psychologist to his conclusion. As police began to look at Surratt, the killing continued.

January 7, 1978

The killer shot fifty-six-year-old steelworker John Shelkons and left Shelkons' wife for dead in their single-story home on McNair Street in Baden. Forty-eight-year-old Catherine "Kay" Shelkons had taken a sleeping pill and was in a deep slumber on the living room couch when she heard a bang, jumped to her feet, and confronted a strange man wearing a bandana over most of his face and holding a shotgun. He told her, "Keep quiet; you're coming with me." When Kay refused and darted for the phone, he attacked her, beating her and kicking her in the face. The next thing she knew the killer was gone and her daughter, who was returning home with a date, stood over her in horror. Police thought her daughter might have frightened the killer away.

Police found the killer had entered through a basement door and climbed the stairs. John Shelkons was watching television and probably heard him approach and met the blast of his shotgun in the hallway at the top of the stairs. Kay Shelkons, her beaten face nearly unrecognizable, told the police she couldn't describe the killer. After much questioning, she remembered tidbits. She said the killer wore a bandana. He had dark hair, but she thought it was a wig. All police had from the crime scene was a man's size 10 shoeprint.

Many people were dead. Most others were afraid they would be next. Kay had to help police find the killer. So despite her groggy state during the attack, she described a white man. Her words led to instant division among the investigating officers. Many gave up on Edward Surratt and began to search for the white man Kay envisioned. Others thought the enormous pressure on Kay elicited an imagined response. Either way, the description crippled the police effort.

March 27, 1978

Police stopped Surratt in Boardman Township, Ohio, for making an illegal left turn directly in front of a police cruiser. The officer cited him and let him go. The next morning, a neighbor noticed Katherine Flicky's home had a broken glass door. Police discovered Flicky, a seventy-year-old widow dead inside. She lived alone in a neat single-story home backed by woods just two miles from the same truck stop near the two sets of Beaver Township murders. Her residence was about one mile from where police had stopped Surratt. Flicky had been beaten to death.

They found Flicky nude in her bathtub. Moisture on her skin made it appear the killer had filled the tub and then allowed it to drain, possibly destroying physical evidence on her body. Police carefully vacuumed the crime scene and found hairs consistent with those of a black man. Police could find no evidence that a black person had visited her home prior to the murder, so they believed the hairs must have been from the killer.

June 1, 1978

Sixty-six-year-old Luther Langford of West Columbia, South Carolina, was found murdered along with his wife, Nell, fifty-eight, who had been severely beaten, sexually assaulted, and left for dead inside their single-story home. South Carolina police put out an alert for their missing vehicle. Surratt's wife, Offia, who had been secretly cooperating with police, notified them that her husband had left a car with South Carolina plates in the West Aliquippa parking lot next to the J&L Steel Corporation plant.

June 6, 1978

When Surratt appeared at the parking lot at 10:20 p.m., undercover troopers attempted to apprehend him. But Surratt led the men, who were weighed down with heavy protective vests, on a chase toward the mill. State police hadn't notified local police about the stakeout, and no immediate backup was available. An undercover vice trooper chased Surratt through the massive mill and lost him when Surratt plunged over a steep and jagged fifty- to sixty-foot drop to the edge of the Ohio River. The search continued well into the night.

Officers debated Surratt's course. Perhaps he had cut back across the mill, over the four lanes of Route 51, and into the dense tangle of homes clinging to an otherwise wooded hillside in the city's Logstown section. Maybe he had sprinted through the half-mile length of the plant and found the opening to a piped stream of storm water snaking beneath Franklin Avenue, Aliquippa's main street. The stream has an eight-foot opening near the Franklin Avenue J&L entrance, plenty large enough for a man to run or even drive through. The tunnel's beginning, a little more than a mile away at the city's Stone Arch area, was a place at which Surratt had played as a child. Others argued that Surratt dived into the Ohio River and swam away. Another theory was that a mill worker sneaked Surratt out. Surratt was familiar with the mill, having delivered steel ingots there many times. Surratt would next turn up in Florida.

July 1, 1978

That night, a man, his wife, and their teenage daughter were held hostage by a black man at their North Beach single-story home. The intruder had fallen asleep, and the father had escaped to a neighbor's house, where he called police. Four officers arrived to find a silent struggle with neighbors holding back the distraught father as he tried to go back into the house and kill the intruder.

The father said the intruder had forced his way into the house earlier that day with a 7 mm Mauser rifle, tied everyone up with electrical cords in the bedroom, and then repeatedly raped his wife and his eighteen-year-old stepdaughter in front of him. Then the intruder drank a bottle of their wine, smoked two marijuana cigarettes, and passed out naked on the bed. The father somehow freed himself and escaped with the gun. Florida police held Surratt for three days before FBI descriptions of Surratt's tattoos, fingerprints, and scars alerted them to who he was. As soon as word got out, officers from nearly every local agency involved headed to the Sunshine State to question him.

Edward Surratt only confessed to and was convicted of killing Luther and Nell Langford of West Columbia, South Carolina. He is the prime suspect in similar unsolved murders on the eastern seaboard. He is currently serving life in a South Carolina prison with enough convictions to keep him locked up for the rest of his natural life.

Police still ask for your help with the unsolved murders of these remaining victims. They have said not to discount the relevance of any information you may know. Your piece of information may have a significant impact on the investigation when viewed in the context of what they already know. For further information, please call the Pennsylvania

State Police at (717) 783-5524, Pittsburgh FBI at (412) 432-4000, or you can E-mail whokilled@rooftoppublishing.com, and we will pass along this information.

Research and development for this story was made possible by the assistance of the Pittsburgh Public Library, *Pittsburgh Post, Tribune-Review, The Beaver County Times* and *The Allegheny Times* newspapers, Pennsylvania State Police, the FBI, and the friends and family of all of these victims.

Who Killed 13-year-old Barbara Ann Barnes?

Like so many other schoolchildren, thirteen-year-old Barbara Barnes, pictured to the left, walked to and from school each day. Her family knew her as "Barbie," but the quiet girl was nothing like the flashy doll of that name. She had been blessed with intelligence, beauty, and friendliness but rarely spoke without being asked a question. Barbara was one of the brightest students in her eighth-grade class at Harding Middle School, where she sang in the choir. Friends recall she rarely spoke to anyone about her family, her poverty, or her father's murder seven years prior to hers. Barbara Ann Barnes keeps her secrets to this day.

On December 7, 1995, Barbara vanished. No one realized she was gone until after 3 p.m. "She usually comes home after school," said Kathy Barnes, her mother, back in 1995. "And she never returned." Her mother had missed phone calls from the school notifying her that Barbara was not there.

The brown-haired, brown-eyed girl was last seen at the intersection of Brady Circle and Ridge Avenue just blocks from where she attended Harding Middle School. Justin Rinehart, a classmate, noticed her walking ahead of him before he became distracted. He didn't see her the next time he looked in her direction. At first, Steubenville police treated her disappearance as a missing person's case. Law enforcement, family, friends, and people who didn't even know Barbara started to search. Police Sergeant Bob Villamagna was in charge of juvenile cases at the time. "Even if I retire I'll never rest until this case is done," he said at the time. Children who walked to school along her route told investigators they couldn't remember whether they'd seen Barbara the morning she disappeared. Once she vanished, the city of about 20,000 could talk of no one else.

Crews roamed wooded areas, riverbanks, and places like Union Cemetery, which sits right behind Barbara's school. But searches turned up nothing. Days turned into weeks and months, but the family remained hopeful she'd return. But then, three months later on February 22, 1996, devastating news traveled back home. Surveyors near Clinton, Pennsylvania, had found a young girl's body. Someone had dug a shallow grave in a creek bed; local police were called to the scene. "The surveyor took one last look at the stakes," said Officer Villamagna. "He wanted to go down the hill and look at these stakes again and make sure everything was the way it was supposed to be. And when he went down over the hill, he saw part of her body exposed."

The search was over. Barbara had been found. Her initial cause of death was strangulation.

Back home, a community mourned and wanted to know how this could have happened to such a young, innocent girl. The case switched from finding Barbara to finding her killer. Police became overwhelmed with leads, calls, and even a psychic who had visions of how the murder happened. "There was a lot of information," Villamagna said. Police questioned suspects, some as far away as the desert southwest. But just when it looked like they were making progress, they hit roadblocks. They were no closer to finding the murderer, which prompted the FBI to offer a $90,000 reward. Now, more than ten years have passed, and the people closest to the case still can't rest.

Villamagna admitted, "I can't think of another crime that's more horrendous than to do something to a child like that. If you can do what they did to that kid, you can do anything to anybody." Barbara Barnes' murder case has been revisited recently as Steubenville police and the Jefferson County Sheriff's Department follow up on new leads. But the critical pieces of evidence are still out there, and law enforcement agencies remain optimistic they'll find them.

"Everyone that's involved in this case is 99.9 percent sure who the perpetrator is but just can't get that one little thing to lock the door on that case," Villamagna said. "Somebody knows something."

Barbara's murdered body lay buried for months in a dry, three-foot-wide creek bed near Pittsburgh International Airport. The final coroner report said she had been strangled to death. During the two and a half months she was missing, hundreds of people crowded Steubenville's streets for candlelight vigils. Children were not allowed to go outside alone, and Barbara's classmates wore yellow ribbons to school. The FBI rented office space in Steubenville, while Findlay and Allegheny County police combed the airport area. No one could find the killer.

A family statement brought it all home for everyone: "It's always the children who pay. You very seldom see a grownup end up like this. I wish I could get out a message to the public that this ought to give every parent in the whole world an idea of what it means to look out for their children."

"It struck a nerve here," said Rob Rembold, then-vice principal of Harding Middle School and now the principal. His son knew Barbara. "It's every parent's worst nightmare.... She was just a very lovely young lady and never bothered anybody. That's why just the circumstances of what happened had everybody uneasy," Rembold said.

More than 300 people attended Barbara's funeral at First Westminster Presbyterian Church in Steubenville. Salvation Army Major Edith Copeland tried to soothe the stricken city by assuring them the murder "will not go unpunished." Most in town have been able to dim the memory of Barbara's disappearance and grisly discovery. Steubenville Police Detective John Stasiulewicz, however, still stays up nights thinking about it. "It's a thing that never leaves you," Stasiulewicz said. "It always feels like the job's not finished."

The case might have caught a break when Florida authorities arrested a man on child abduction charges. Detectives in Florida retraced his movements over the last decade or so and found he had been in Steubenville around the time of Barbara's abduction. Stasiulewicz had tracked his movements when the accused man returned to Ohio several years afterward. If Florida police convict the suspect, Stasiulewicz plans to send a DNA sample to be compared to that of Florida's man. The detective refused to disclose the suspect's identity when he's this close to possibly making an arrest. "I'd like to solve this and let the city know that he'll spend the rest of his natural life in a state penitentiary," Stasiulewicz said.

Jefferson County, Ohio, Sheriff Fred Abdalla, Stasiulewicz, and others suspect someone much closer to Barbara somehow played a role in her death. Some theorize the Florida man had

nothing to do with the slaying. Barbara's body wa
one and a half miles of a farm owned by a re
Boyce, Barbara's uncle. Investigators took so
shovels found on that property, but they didn't match
the creek bed where Barbara's body was found.

Boyce was given a lie-detector test. "He flunked the
polygraph miserably," Abdalla said. But those test results are not
admissible as court evidence. Stasiulewicz said he first became
suspicious of Louis Boyce and his wife, Mary, when they hired
a lawyer to represent them early in the investigation of the
case. "I can't understand why a member of the family would get
an attorney," Stasiulewicz said. From their home in Midland,
Beaver County, Mary Boyce told a *Tribune-Review* reporter that
interview requests had to go through their attorney, Columbus,
Ohio, lawyer Gary W. Deeds. Deeds relayed the interview
request back to the Boyces.

"He said I don't have to talk to you if I don't want to," Mary
Boyce said after a subsequent phone call with the newspaper
reporter. "I don't have nothing to say." James Montgomery, a
friend of Louis Boyce who still lives in Steubenville, laughed
at police accusations of Boyce hiding something. "That's a
bunch of crap. Louis would never hurt any one of those kids,"
Montgomery said, referring to Barbara, her sister Melissa, and
her brother Gary. Police questioned Montgomery in Barbara's
disappearance, and they suspected him of playing a role in the
murder of Barbara's father, Gary Barnes, in 1989. Mike Dugan,
a friend of Montgomery and Gary Barnes, is serving a life
sentence for the slaying.

Montgomery was one of the last to see Gary Barnes, thirty-
seven, when the two had "one or two beers" at an American
Legion near both men's homes the night of his murder. "He
said he had to go home and he left," Montgomery said. "Kathy

rnes [Gary's wife] called family members the next morning and said, 'They shot Gary.'" Accounts differ on the relationship between Montgomery and Kathy Barnes. Montgomery said the two were friends.

Kathy Barnes, a soft-spoken woman who police describe as "slow," said she only vaguely remembers Montgomery as someone who occasionally lent Gary Barnes his van. "I don't talk to him," she said. Stasiulewicz and Abdalla, however, said informants told them Montgomery and Kathy Barnes began a romantic relationship around the time her husband was shot. Nearly seven years later, in the days before Barbara's abduction, a van that looked like Montgomery's Ford Econoline was spotted around the Barnes home, Stasiulewicz said. "They're just trying to cover a case and trying to get anyone they can get," Montgomery said.

Since an interview with the *Tribune-Review*, Montgomery died of natural causes. Kathy Barnes, during an interview in her home in a Steubenville public housing development, said she doesn't believe a relative or friend kidnapped her daughter. In the next breath, however, she said she doesn't think her daughter would have gotten into a car with someone she did not know.

"If it was a stranger who picked her up, did she struggle? Why didn't anybody see it?" asked Pete Basil, assistant superintendent of Steubenville's school district and the former principal of Barbara's middle school. "Why go way out into the woods, in another state, and bury her? Whatever happened that person felt he had to dispose of the body in a way that didn't come back to Steubenville."

Family and friends say thirteen-year-old Barbara had changed during her final few months. Memories of her father began to resurface frequently and clearly, causing Barbara to cry a lot more often. "Barbie was attached to her dad," Basil said. "She was daddy's girl." No one has been charged with her murder.

Police still ask for your help with the unsolved murder of Barbara Barnes. They have said not to discount the relevance of any information you may know. Your piece of information may have a significant impact on the investigation when viewed in the context of what they already know. For further information, call the Steubenville police at (740) 283-6000, or you can E-mail whokilled@rooftoppublishing.com, and we will pass along this information.

Research and development for this story was made possible by the assistance of the Pittsburgh Public Library, *Pittsburgh Post* and *Tribune-Review* newspapers, Steubenville police, and the friends and family of Barbara.

Who Killed John Yelenic the Day Before His Divorce?

Thirty-nine-year-old John Yelenic, pictured to the left, was on top of the world as a successful dentist and partner in the Reilly & Yelenic Dental Office on Market Street in small-town Blairsville, Pennsylvania. Pulling up to his South Springs Street home on April 12, 2006, he may have noticed the kids' bikes parked in a row and how the shade from the trees not only kept the front of his residence cool in the summer months but also partially hid its front view from the rest of the neighborhood.

The only stress in his life was the five-year rocky separation from wife Michelle—a reported stormy split including his arrest in 2003 for violating a protective order she had placed against him for alleged abuse. During happier times of their marriage, John and Michelle adopted a baby boy, "Jay-Jay," while visiting Russia. Their seven-year-old son was now the last remaining tie to each parent. It was no secret John wanted custody of Jay-Jay, but Michelle refused. During their rocky separation, Michelle had once tried to have John arrested for molesting his son. After a police investigation, it was determined the charges were unfounded. Now everything had worked its way out and their divorce was final except for the judge's signature that would occur the next day.

Later that evening, an upbeat Yelenic called an aunt, Ruth Carlson, to tell her that his divorce had been granted and how happy he was to be able to get on with his life. "You're not going to believe what I'm holding in my hand," Yelenic told Carlson. "The divorce?" his aunt replied. "This is what I've been waiting years for," Yelenic said. According to Carlson, "He said, 'My next goal is to get custody of my son.' He just couldn't wait to see him."

Later the same evening, neighbors said they heard loud noises like fighting coming from the direction of John's home. Dogs were also heard barking, but no one called the police. Yelenic had not been sleeping well at night and would stay downstairs in the living room watching TV on the couch and occasionally nursing a drink until he dozed off. It's not known if he were sleeping downstairs this night or not.

The next day, a child noticed a broken window and some blood on the area of the front door at Yelenic's house and summoned two other people, who opened the door and found Yelenic's body. If the brick house could talk, it would describe a violent tale of its owner being murdered by someone who likely knew John because there were no signs of forced entry. Once inside, a terrible fight broke out that spilled over into two separate rooms and produced a fatal cut to the dentist's throat police believe occurred when his head crashed through a plate-glass window. His attacker fled, leaving John Yelenic bleeding to death.

Blairsville Police Chief Donald Hess said Dr. Yelenic was targeted by the killer, not the victim of a random burglar. "There are multiple wounds on the body, but we do not know what they were made with yet." He described the area surrounding Yelenic's body as one of disarray. Police do believe Yelenic knew his killer because he let him into his home that night. His body, clad in a T-shirt and sweatpants, was found just inside the front door.

Police collected blood for DNA testing and asked the Pennsylvania state police to probe into the details of Yelenic's private and professional life. The FBI even created a computerized version of Yelenic's home using laser beams to map the layout of the crime scene to help understand what happened. Chief Hess stated they would make an arrest. The county coroner said the dentist had injuries from an apparent violent struggle and ruled his death a homicide. "Although the coroner's office cannot release certain details of the autopsy because of the ongoing investigation, I am fully convinced of homicide in Dr. Yelenic's death," Indiana County Coroner Michael Baker said.

Days later, a strip of sheet metal covered the broken glass. Witnesses saw an outline of a bloody footprint on the wooden floor in the foyer. There also were fresh bloodstains on the fireplace wall in the adjoining living room. Yelenic's cousin Mary Ann Clark of Blairsville walked reporters through the house and reportedly hesitated when she reached for a knob on the back door. "The killer likely touched it when he fled. State police and federal forensic experts combed the entire home, testing bloody carpeting, draperies, the rear sidewalk and even the back doorknob looking for clues." She went on to explain, "We've changed all the locks, except this one." Just the sight of the home's interior rekindles her pain. "Blood was everywhere," Clark said. "It was under the window. There was blood by the fireplace. The carpet was soaked with blood."

Clark also pointed out that John kept three rifles in the basement and a handgun upstairs. There were no signs he tried to get those weapons on the night he was killed. "That tells me he wasn't expecting any problems."

Neighbors, friends, and relatives began talking amongst themselves, and the general comments focused on a link between John's murder and divorce. Facts emerging indicated a very messy separation that included documents on file at the Indiana County Courthouse suggesting over time the divorce grew increasingly nasty. The Yelenics were married on December 31, 1997, in Las Vegas. According to court records, they separated four years later. John Yelenic filed for divorce in 2002. His wife filed divorce papers the following year. The couple apparently agreed in the beginning to joint custody of their son. As divorces go, their joint agreements soon became hostile disagreements.

Michelle Yelenic was cited by Judge Hanna for contempt of court in October 2004 and ordered to pay a $1,000 fine. The contempt charge stemmed from removing her son from public school and placing him in a private parochial school without first seeking her husband's approval. In May 2005, Michelle Yelenic filed for a protection from abuse order against her husband, claiming he sexually abused their son during a visit with him a month earlier.

According to court documents, Indiana County Children and Youth Services investigated and ruled the complaint was unfounded. In court documents, John Yelenic contended that his wife fabricated the abuse allegations as a means to alienate him from his son. In October of the same year, Hanna ordered the Yelenics and their son to attend family counseling. Meanwhile, the divorce was moving forward. John Yelenic asked the court to finalize the divorce because he and his wife had lived apart for more than two years.

But then Michelle Yelenic seemed to have second thoughts. She filed a legal notice in which she opposed the divorce, claiming their marriage was "not irretrievably broken." However, court records indicate that in January the Yelenics and their lawyers met informally and reached a handshake agreement about how to divide the family assets that would enable the divorce to move forward.

That agreement called for Michelle Yelenic to receive a reduction in monthly child-support payments from $3,875 to $1,337 from her husband. John agreed to pay his wife more than $54,000 for her share of several properties the couple jointly owned as well as a portion of his dental practice. Michelle Yelenic also was to receive more than $38,000 from an annuity they held while her husband agreed to pay for her Blairsville home and for their son's medical expenses and school tuition.

With the police investigation unable to identify any viable suspects outside of the immediate family, they turned their focus on John's last will and testament for motive. Police confirmed the will was seized from Yelenic's safe and stated details about its contents remained guarded, but Yelenic's attorney said he was in the process of altering it. Effie Alexander, who was handling Yelenic's divorce from his estranged wife, said John's will was just one part of the doctor's estate that was being questioned by police. "He was in the process of completing a new will, but he had not finalized it to my knowledge. We talked about drafting a new will repeatedly, but I'm not sure that he did it," Alexander said.

Michelle quickly made efforts to have her final divorce decree signed by a judge even though her husband was now dead. A legal battle ensued that set a legal precedent in Pennsylvania and caught the attention of courts and newswire services across the country. At one point, Court TV attempted to air a segment on the Yelenic's unique dilemma. The legal dispute Michelle was trying to avoid revolved around a January 2005 amendment to the state's divorce code and the implications of a two-part divorce, one in which the divorce decree is issued separately from a property settlement. If she could get the decree signed off on by a judge, Michelle could then enforce the original divorce settlement while her son would become legal heir to John's estate.

A two-part divorce is used, for example, when a person wants to remarry without having to wait for the property settlement, which is often far more complicated to be resolved. An expert in Pennsylvania family law says there was no reason to declare a dead man divorced because the dentist's wife and adopted son would receive support under the property settlement, which legally overrides his will.

"What difference does the decree really make?" said Pittsburgh attorney Jay Blechman, chairman of the family law section of the Pennsylvania Bar Association. "As far as I can tell, there isn't a difference."

John's attorney held to a desire to have a judge make a ruling nonetheless. "We are, along with the estate attorney, conducting research to determine if there's any significance to the decree being denied." Attorney Alexander stated her reasoning: "From my perspective, this is what John wanted. You know how people say after someone is dead, 'If there was one thing I could do for him now'? Well, this is really a personal thing for me and my law firm."

On July 26, 2006, the court denied the request saying a dead man cannot obtain a divorce in Pennsylvania. Common

Pleas Judge Carol Hanna refused the request by attorneys to grant a posthumous divorce. If the request had been granted, Yelenic's divorce would have been cited as a landmark case in Pennsylvania. The Pennsylvania Superior Court upheld the local judge's ruling on April 17 of this year.

As of this date, there have been no arrests in Doctor Yelenic's case. Since his death, Clark and Yelenic's friends have pressured police for details and offered the names of possible suspects. They've offered a reward and tried to interest television crime shows in the case. A Ligonier filmmaker is making a documentary about the life of the small-town dentist. Mary Ann Clark stated in a December 2006 interview with the *Tribune-Review* that she and Yelenic's friends are frustrated by the pace of the investigation by the Pennsylvania State Police and the secrecy surrounding the probe. Yelenic's friends have now contacted Geraldo Rivera, Nancy Grace, *Dateline NBC, 48 Hours* on CBS, and *America's Most Wanted*, trying to get some exposure of John's murder. In August, they put up a booth at Blairsville Diamond Days to urge anyone with information about the killing to contact police.

The reward fund has grown to nearly $15,000 for the arrest and conviction of Yelenic's killer. Relatives, friends, patients, members of his church, and fellow dentists have donated the money. Dennis Vaughn, a college classmate who lives in Winchester, Virginia, said he contacted *Dateline* and *America's Most Wanted* out of frustration. "I haven't gotten a whole lot of feedback from police," Vaughn said. "There's a big debate with me and my other college friends in wondering how long is too long. I have gotten to the point where I will wait at least until the first of the year and hope we get a break."

Clark said Blairsville police have not been forthcoming about the investigation because they told them they consider everybody a suspect. "They plead with us for patience. We're holding on to that. When I really get mad, they finally say at the end of this, 'We don't want to sit across the table and say we're sorry' they couldn't solve the case. They keep telling us they're narrowing the field," Vaughn added. "We've heard a lot of rumors but very little official word."

Dennis Laverich, of Philadelphia, another college friend of Yelenic's, said, "I'm so disgusted that my will has been broken." Laverich said he gave police information pointing to potential suspects. Laverich said Yelenic had told him about some personal problems he was having before his death and about threats and intimidation he had faced. He said friends have remained quiet about the case, honoring police requests not to talk to reporters. But Laverich said he's no longer willing to remain silent. "We feel we've been duped into being quiet," he said. "We want to put pressure on the police. That's why we contacted these national programs."

Police still ask for your help with the unsolved murder of Dr. John Yelenic. They have said not to discount the relevance of any information you may know. Your piece of information may have a significant impact on the investigation when viewed in the context of what they already know. For further information, call Blairsville police at (724) 459-7555, or you can E-mail whokilled@rooftoppublishing.com, and we will pass along this information.

Research and development for this story was made possible by the assistance of the Pittsburgh Public Library, *Pittsburgh Post* and *Tribune-Review* newspapers, Pittsburgh police, and the friends and family of Dr. Yelenic.

Who Killed Catherine Corkery?

Eighteen years have passed since Catherine Corkery, pictured to the left, a Mt. Lebanon High School graduate and Dormont resident, was beaten, strangled, sexually assaulted, stabbed then set on fire before her remains were discovered the morning of Saturday, July 22, 1989. Her father called her killer "a son of a bitch" in a 2005 *Pittsburgh Tribune* newspaper article.

According to news stories and authorities, it took sixteen hours to identify her. They relied on fingerprints and dental records. She was found under a cherry tree, two blocks from her Dormont home. The flames that consumed her naked upper body flared so high they scorched the tree's limbs. The neighbors couldn't stand to look at that tree, a constant reminder of such a heinous death, so they chopped it down a few days later, said David Corkery, the victim's father. "Sometimes you think if we would have lost Cathy to a car accident, I think it would have been easier," said Rebecca Finney, a high school friend of Corkery's. "The thought of her suffering, the thought of what she went through before she died, it really tears me up."

Cathy, Rebecca, and another friend enjoyed drinks that Friday night, July 21, at a Mt. Lebanon bar before meeting Corkery's boyfriend, Tim Rooney, and Finney's boyfriend at a party. Rooney, who planned to someday ask Corkery to marry him, left early because he had a painting job the next morning. Corkery mentioned several times that night that she planned to walk home, but Rooney and Finney said Corkery finally relented and agreed to get a ride with a friend. No one knows for sure what she did. According to news accounts, after Rooney left, Finney was dealt into a poker game. "One of the guys left and let me play his hand until he came back," Finney said. "I did really well. That's the only time in my life that I've played well. Otherwise, I would have been hanging out with Cathy." Rooney awoke the next morning to find himself alone in the Ordinance Avenue apartment he shared with Corkery. He assumed she spent the night at a friend's.

Rooney said he returned home Saturday afternoon and began to worry. It was only after hearing a 6 p.m. newscast reporting that a body had been found near his apartment that Rooney believed Corkery was dead. "It was terrifying," Rooney said. "Look at the brutality of it. It's animal-like." Police questioned everyone who attended the party but found few clues. Rooney still visits Corkery's grave. "Quite frankly, it's still very hard to handle," he said to reporters. "There's no set recipe for getting over tragedy, the pain kind of goes away after awhile. You know she's not coming back. You just hope to God that they find the perpetrator."

Unknown to Cathy's father, friends, and law enforcement is whether she fell victim to the pattern of a spree killer along with seven additional women from at least 1984 through 1991. During this time, eight young women who shared similarities were killed in the same fashion. All were beaten, stabbed, and sexually assaulted then doused with a flammable liquid while still alive. FBI and multiple other police agencies banded together in 1991 to investigate the similarities and probability that the same man murdered these girls—the same man who has to date not been captured. Or has he?

1. <u>On July 17, 1984</u>, California authorities found the charred body of an unidentified young woman along Interstate 80 near Squaw Valley. She had been stabbed, bound, doused with kerosene, and set on fire while still alive.

2. <u>On July 16, 1985</u>, Virginia Beach police found the charred remains of twenty-year-old Raffaella Bryant in a burnt-out vehicle located in a cornfield.

3. <u>On September 26, 1986</u>, Maryland State Police found twenty-nine-year-old Brenda Bloom dead in a park near the Baltimore-Washington Airport. She too had been stabbed and set on fire while still alive.

4. <u>On July 22, 1989</u>, Dormont, Pennsylvania, police found the body of twenty-two-year-old Catherine Corkery, who had been stabbed, sexually assaulted, doused with a flammable liquid, and set on fire while still alive.

5. <u>On April 16, 1990</u>, Huttonville, Ontario, police found the body of twenty-one-year-old Lynda Shaw, who had been severely beaten, stabbed repeatedly, doused with a flammable liquid, and set on fire while still alive.

6. <u>On November 14, 1990</u>, Ohio police found thirty-two-year-old Elaine Graham of Hambden Township sitting in the passenger seat of her car that was engulfed in flames after being doused with a flammable liquid.

7. <u>On December 14, 1990</u>, Ohio police found thirty-seven-year-old Jean Eddy of Lakewood dead in her burning car parked in a cornfield after being doused with a flammable liquid. The coroner ruled her death a suicide even though Lakewood police aren't sure they agree with that ruling. Family and friends say she was murdered. Police commented it is very unusual for a woman to commit suicide by setting herself on fire.

8. <u>On March 19, 1991</u>, Ohio police found the body of twenty-three-year-old Rachael Johnson of Tallmadge lying in the street near Akron. She had been stabbed repeatedly, sexually assaulted, and first thrown from a moving vehicle and then doused with a flammable liquid and set on fire while still alive. Rachael's murder was profiled in *Who Killed ...? Cleveland*.

"What is unique about all of these cases is the amount of pain the killer inflicts," said Akron, Ohio, Detective Bruce Van Horn. In several of the killings, the women were beaten, stabbed in the chest and face to the point of mutilation, raped, and, while they were still alive, set on fire. "I can't think of a more painful way to die," Van Horn said.

Police have not been able to arrest anyone for Catherine Corkery's murder, nor any of the women listed who were tortured then murdered. Or have they and just don't know it?

Was this the work of a traveling, crazed, sadistic killer? Take for instance convicted cross-country spree killer Glen Edward Rogers, pictured on the next page, who bragged of

killing over fifty people, mostly women. Rogers grew up in Hamilton, Ohio, and boasted to friends and family of torture-style murders from Ohio to California in the early nineties. Born July 19, 1962, in Hamilton, Ohio, near Cincinnati, Rogers now sits on Florida's death row, having been convicted and sentenced to death in both California and Florida for murder. From the time he was old enough to be arrested, Rogers was getting in trouble with the law. At eighteen, he was picked up at least five times in his hometown of Hamilton for offenses as serious as aggravated menacing and as minor as having no muffler on his car.

Ohio police say they lost track of him from 1982 to when he resurfaced in 1987. When he returned to Hamilton, they started arresting him again. In 1987, he was charged three times for public intoxication in Hamilton and once for drunken driving in Richmond, Kentucky. Police can only speculate where he was while gone for four years, but it's believed he ended up in California before returning home. In the 1980s, Hamilton was the only Ohio jurisdiction to send Rogers to state prison on forgery and breaking-and-entering charges. On November 9, 1987, Rogers tried to ram his car through the Midas Muffler Shop's plate-glass window. He stole a blank check and filled it in for $450.

He was sentenced to two years in jail, the maximum. After being paroled and violating his parole, Rogers was released for good on June 1, 1989.

Glen Rogers left Ohio again in or about 1993, ending up in Los Angeles by the end of the next year. Most people who knew him stated he was the type of person who could talk you into doing anything he wanted. Joining the traveling carnival network and working for Farrow Amusement and Charles Companies provided him a means to travel from town to town all across the United States. His murdering spree began to surface in the early nineties, but no one really knows when it may have started. Several books have been written about Glen Rogers outlining his killing spree in at least the nineties. His infamous torture-style killing may have begun long before 1992.

Could this cold-blooded killer have been involved in Catherine Corkery's murder? And what of the other seven women? The time frame, locations, and his admitted brutal style of murdering women (at least one of his victims being set on fire in the 1990s) make it a real possibility. It is a fact that he had family in Canada where Lynda Shaw was severely beaten, stabbed, and doused with a flammable liquid in 1990. The one solid clue that points to Rogers as a possible suspect is the fact that during the same time period he was knowingly back in Ohio, and while he was in prison from 1987 until his release in June of 1989, there were no murders committed fitting this profile. Then one month after his June release from custody, Catherine Corkery was murdered in Dormont, Pennsylvania.

His recorded cross-country murder spree is documented beginning in late 1992. In 1994, he admitted to one of his family members that he had just killed someone and, in fact, had already "killed at least 8 people." Part of his MO was seeking out women in bars and nightclubs. The last night Catherine Corkery was alive, she and friends were at a local bar, and no one knows when she left, whether she left by herself, or how she was going to get home. There are only two things they know for sure. First, Catherine was severely beaten, stabbed, sexually assaulted then set on fire to die. Second, no arrests have ever been made.

As for Glen Rogers, in the end one of his own relatives near Waco, Kentucky, turned him in when he made a personal appearance asking for money and help. She said she loved her younger cousin and it hurt to turn him in, but "he had to be stopped."

After his high-speed chase and arrest in November of 1995 by Kentucky police, Rogers, pictured to the left, confessed and even boasted of his murderous career to law enforcement and the media. At first, Rogers loved the media attention, making statements that he had killed up to seventy people and that his days with the carnivals paved the way for him to go town to town luring young women to their deaths. At some time during his TV debut and with the thought of being put to death, Rogers did a quick turnaround and said he never killed anyone. It was "just a joke."

Florida and California juries did not see the humor, and both states sentenced him to die for his crimes. Now sitting on death row, Glen Rogers, pictured to the right, enjoys being able to taunt the police, courts, and the

media with his prison Web pages provided by the Canadian Coalition Against The Death Penalty, or CCADP. It is an organization that may have had good intentions in their pursuit and belief against the death penalty, but for this convicted killer, they have provided him with a life in the outside world to advertise and invite people to "Contact Glen Directly" as pen pals. His personal bio and other information are listed along with family pictures and essays on his feelings ranging from the justice system to his personal life—all of which seems to take away from the idea of "death row" for a man who once boasted of killing over "70" people.

Police still ask for your help with the unsolved murder of Catherine Corkery or any of the other victims portrayed in this chapter. They have said not to discount the relevance of any information you may know. Your piece of information may have a significant impact on the investigation when viewed in the context of what they already know. For further information, call Dormont police at (412) 561-8900, or you can E-mail whokilled@rooftoppublishing.com, and we will pass along this information.

Research and development for this story was made possible by the assistance of the Pittsburgh Public Library, *Pittsburgh Post* and *Tribune-Review* newspapers, Pittsburgh police, and the friends and family of Catherine.

Who Is the Washington County Strangler?

Is there such a thing as mirrored circumstances? If so, it first occurred in the Washington County, Pennsylvania, area in 1977 when six young women were strangled to death in just six months. One hundred thirty miles away and ten years later, four women in the Summit County, Ohio, area were murdered in just under five months. All eleven deaths will leave citizens, police, and both counties' officials baffled. Is there a connection, or is it just a grisly coincidence?

In Washington County, a vicious murder spree targeting young women thirty years ago prompted people to lock doors they once left open. Gun sales soared, and self-defense classes were organized. Women left their homes with escorts or notified loved ones when they arrived safely at their destinations. Residents tuned in to television newscasts and read newspaper coverage to learn details about savage murders of the type that more often occur on urban streets. But the question persists: Who killed all six women from November 1976 to May 1977?

Over the years, police and residents speculated the likes of Ted Bundy or Edward Surratt, among other noted serial killers, might have looped through the county on a killing spree. But clues were lacking, and local residents and some police concluded a "Washington Strangler" was responsible for all six killings. Police conducted exhaustive investigations for years then finally set them aside in frustration, some still feeling the need to capture the fiend who eluded them for nearly three decades. Police thought they had their serial killer in 2000 when David Robert Kennedy, forty-eight, of Cecil, Pennsylvania, was arrested, tried, and convicted through DNA for the March 17, 1977, rape and strangulation murder of Deborah Jeannette Capiola, seventeen, of Findlay. Forensic evidence failed to conclusively point them towards Kennedy for the other five victims.

Barbara Jean Lewis, thirty, was found November 17, 1976, strangled to death in a trash container outside the Brackenridge Civic Association in Churchill, Allegheny County, about a mile from her Penn Hills home. Like the victims that would follow, she was partially clad and her other belongings were found less than two miles from her remains.

Her sister last saw Lewis at about 6:15 a.m. as she was preparing to walk to the bus stop, less than a five-minute walk from the Lewis home. Her remains, still warm, were found around 9 a.m. by a cleaning woman at the civic association. She was strangled by hand, but her killer had stuffed her mouth and nostrils tightly with paper gauze after death. There was no sign of sexual assault, although Lewis's underwear was on inside out and her bra was askew and torn. Police were left clueless, even after an exhausting investigation and hundreds of interviews. Churchill Police Chief Richard James was a patrolman at the time. "We had a number of suspects, but nothing ever came of it," said James.

<u>Susan Rush</u>, twenty-one, vanished at about 6:10 p.m. on November 24, 1976, after leaving her job at Murphy's department store in the Washington Mall in South Strabane. Her body was found shortly after 9 a.m. the next day when her brother Gary Rush spotted her vehicle parked along North Avenue less than a mile from the mall. Her car doors were locked, and her body was in the trunk clad in pants and a turtleneck that was inside out. Rush had been strangled with a piece of string or leather, according to the autopsy report. There were no bruises or scratches on the body, except for the ligature marks, and tests showed that Rush had had sex shortly before her death, which occurred about midnight. If she submitted to sex, it was only to save her life, according to Rush's family. She was a deeply religious person who never had been on a date.

<u>Mary Irene Gency</u>, sixteen, of North Charleroi, disappeared on February 13, 1977, when she left home after dinner to meet some friends. Her severely beaten and frozen body was found six days later in a secluded, wooded section of Fallowfield. She was raped and died from multiple skull fractures and brain lacerations. Although police arrested David Davoli, nineteen, several months later, he was released when prosecutors failed to establish evidence against him, except that Gency may have been seen in his car ninety minutes before her death. Mary had not been strangled, but authorities feel the close time frame of all the murders and close proximity of their bodies to each other indicates they are related.

<u>Deborah Jeannette Capiola</u>, seventeen, of Findlay, Pennsylvania, vanished the morning of March 17, 1977, on her way to catch the school bus. Her brother usually walked with her but not that day. She left her home on Point Park Road at 7:45

a.m. When the bus arrived eight minutes later, there was no sign of her. Her body was discovered ten days later on a hillside near an abandoned strip mine, about three miles from her home in Robinson, Allegheny County. She had been sexually assaulted, then strangled with the leg of her blue jeans.

David Kennedy became a suspect when his maroon vehicle with a vinyl top was seen speeding near Capiola's home and the crime scene the morning of the murder. He arrived late for work, telling co-workers he had a flat tire. He allegedly later told police he was late because he had visited a local car dealership. Two days before Capiola's remains were found, police searched the spillway of nearby Blue Lake, where some youngsters had found Capiola's belongings. State game wardens said they had spotted Kennedy's vehicle at the lake twice that day. Several days after the homicide, a co-worker said he saw Kennedy removing the vinyl top from his car.

According to news accounts and police records, State Police Trooper Rebecca Loving spearheaded the effort to analyze the DNA in 2000, when she and other members of a cold-case squad came up with the sperm sample on Capiola's blue jeans. She believed Kennedy was watching Capiola walk to her bus in the mornings. "He was a stalker," Loving said. "Her brother would go with her every day. Kennedy knew she was alone that day. He stalked her." Stalking is a typical sign of predatory behavior, and that's a bad omen, according to Loving. "He was a predator," Loving said. "And they don't stop."

Kennedy, married three times with no children, "fits the profile of a serial killer to a tee," she said. Loving requested travel vouchers from the federal government, which employed Kennedy as a civilian mechanic at the 911th Airlift Wing of the Air Force Reserve base in Moon, Allegheny County. "Many times, he was out of state," she said. Most disturbing were

Kennedy's alleged actions in 2000. When Kennedy found out he was being investigated by state police, Loving said he began stalking her.

Trooper Loving said that during a meeting with the suspect, Kennedy leaned toward her and in a casual and conversational voice told her he'd been following her, naming places she'd been recently and details of what she wore on certain days. She believes he followed her on at least two occasions. "He scared the hell out of me," she said. On the day Kennedy was arrested, Loving had mixed feelings of accomplishment and grief. "I just cried like a baby," she said.

Kennedy was convicted and sentenced to life.

Brenda Lee Ritter of North Strabane was found strangled in scrub woods within several miles of her home. The eighteen-year-old secretary left her boyfriend's home about 10:10 p.m. on May 18, 1977. Her boyfriend, Larry Bonazza, and his mother watched Ritter drive away, making sure her car doors were locked.

The rash of murders had Ritter's family on edge; like many others, they insisted their four daughters lock their car doors and be wary of strangers. The next morning, Brenda's abandoned car was found in neighboring South Strabane. A massive search was organized, but before it could get underway, searchers in a state police helicopter spotted Ritter's remains on a hillside about three-quarters of a mile from her car. Ritter was raped then garroted with her panties, which were twisted tightly around her neck with a stick.

The Ritter investigation seemed to be a turning point for authorities. Why would a young woman, who knew there was a killer on the loose, open her car door or stop for a stranger? At least one detective forwarded a theory that the killer may have been posing as a policeman to gain victims' trust. "We were living in our own little world until somebody invaded it," said Ritter's mother, Hazel Ritter.

Sister Roberta "Robin" Elam was not actually a nun yet on June 13, 1977. The twenty-six-year-old woman was a pre-novitiate candidate. On the day of her murder, she was preparing a silent retreat at the "Mother House" by the order she intended to join for a life in Christ. Roberta Elam was probably by herself in the field by the convent for the Sisters of Mt. St. Joseph to contemplate the commitment she was about to make.

According to regional newspaper accounts published shortly after her death, it appeared that while Roberta was kneeling to pray, she was attacked, raped, then strangled to death by hand and left near an overturned park bench. Her brutal rape and murder occurred within earshot of the Speidel Golf Course, but no one there heard a thing.

A sister in the Order of Mt. St. Joseph was mentioned in news stories explaining why she felt Roberta might have been out in that field near the golf course. "It is always peaceful and quiet there."

Now-retired West Virginia State Police homicide investigator Don Shade was called to lead the investigation two weeks after the murder. By the time he saw the murder scene, Shade said, "cigarette ashes were all over the place," and the chances of obtaining any forensic evidence were slim. Even two weeks after the murder, an area of nearby weeds remained mashed down, indicating the killer had lain in wait for her. Shade said Elam's killer was "very strong" and crushed her larynx. Police obtained blood samples from everyone they could think of, from golfers to priests, and tried hypnosis on witnesses.

The strain felt by public officials became evident after the Elam murder when officials began to publicly criticize then-Washington County district attorney Jesse Costa for not asking the FBI for assistance. The feud intensified with open-aired complaints back and forth with accusations against the prosecutor and law enforcement. Protesters began rallying outside the county courthouse. Police were under scrutiny for not combining resources more effectively and chastised by some victims' families.

A two-part newspaper article written in September 2003 by Janice Crompton for the *Pittsburgh Post-Gazette* details the string of murders, similarities, and their locations. The information Crompton gathered, as well as other research, shows each victim was raped. Debra Capiola appears to have not been penetrated even though sperm was found on her body, causing police to theorize she was still sexually assaulted, and only her murder has been linked to now-convicted David Kennedy. All were either bludgeoned or strangled or both, and except for Sister Elam, the murders appear to have occurred in one place then their bodies disposed of somewhere else.

In the 2003 article recapping the mystery, it is implied that the spree never ceased, per se; it simply moved on, and authorities had spotted similar unsolved crimes in other parts of West Virginia and Ohio as well. Even killers like Ted Bundy and a lesser-known serial killer at the time named Edward Surratt were tested, but they didn't match the still-unsolved murders either.

During this time, police and newspaper accounts referred to the killer as "a maniac," "deranged," and as a "madman" for his evil bravado and cleverness. In a *Pittsburgh Post* story in September of 2003, a former FBI profiler stated that serial killers are "heavily into a fantasy world," according to Robert K.

Ressler, a sixteen-year veteran of the FBI's Behavioral Science Unit. Ressler also is one of the developers of the bureau's violent criminal apprehension program known as VICAP. Ressler now is a private consultant specializing in serial and sexual homicides. He has assisted in investigations of serial killers including Ted Bundy, Charles Manson, Jeffrey Dahmer, and John Wayne Gacy.

In this rash of murders facing authorities as a possible serial killer, Ressler said, "Serial killers have a sense of omnipotence; they become bolder as they go." People like this "develop a style of getting victims." Local authorities who did not believe the area murders were linked often cited the varying methods of strangulation. "It's a common misconception, though, that serial killers follow the same rituals," Ressler said. "These people are experimenters who try many variations."

However, typical serial killers tend to stick with what works in regard to secondary chores, like the way they dispose of a body or lure victims. "This person has to have a skilled way of obtaining victims," Ressler said. One common thread that continues to baffle police is the fact that victims were not bruised, beaten, or otherwise injured during such violent assaults. Some theorized the killer may have used a ruse that he had a flat tire, swiftly shoving victims into his trunk before they knew what was happening or before he drew the attention of passersby. "This case sounds like it could be expanded quite a bit," Ressler said of the local murders.

If the cases are the work of a serial killer, Ressler said it would be a "very organized offender" who chooses his victims and stalks them first. Killers oftentimes return to the scenes of their crimes to relive their fantasies or simply to clean up loose ends, he said. "This is a pattern that we see frequently with serial killers."

The murders continue to haunt the original investigators. South Strabane Police Chief Donald Zofchak said while there were suspects in the Ritter case, including a sketch of a suspect seen walking along nearby Interstate 70 on the night of the murder, nothing panned out. "We never got a good grasp," he said. "It never got to a point where we had anyone zeroed in." State police have taken over the Ritter investigation, and although they have a DNA sample from Ritter's body, it isn't sufficient for testing yet.

To consider a link between the strangulation murders in Pennsylvania and the Summit County, Ohio, murders of four women, you have to look at the locations by the interstate routes. True, interstates are everywhere and could easily be discounted as a true coincidence, but figure the interstate routes in with the possible date patterns and it is hard not to wonder if a serial killer had a job that would keep him on the road at regular intervals.

Police still ask for your help with the unsolved murders of these victims. They have said not to discount the relevance of any information you may know. Your piece of information may have a significant impact on the investigation when viewed in the context of what they already know. For further information, call Pennsylvania State Police at (717) 783-5524, or you can E-mail whokilled@rooftoppublishing.com, and we will pass along this information.

Research and development for this story was made possible by the assistance of the Pittsburgh Public Library, *Pittsburgh Post* and *Tribune-Review* newspapers, Pittsburgh police, and the friends and family of all of these young women.

Who Killed Jamie Lynn Stickle?

Thirty-three-year-old Jamie Stickle, pictured to the left, had finished her shift as a manager at Side Kicks around midnight on February 8, 2002, on Liberty Avenue, Downtown Pittsburgh. Owner David Morrow said she was in a good mood when he last saw her walk across the street and down the block for a drink at Pegasus, another of Morrow's businesses, where she stayed until about 1:15 a.m. She was seen later back across Liberty Avenue at a club called the House of Tilden around 2:45 a.m., but she was denied entrance there because she was said to be drunk. The next time Stickle was seen, she was dead. Firefighters were called at 3:47 a.m. for a vehicle fire in the parking lot of George Warhola Scrap Metal, 203 Chesbro Street, North Side, where Stickle rented an apartment.

Stickle's Jeep was sitting in the same spot it always was, directly in front of the door leading to her second-floor apartment. Jamie was found burned beyond recognition sitting in her vehicle. And despite a $20,000 reward for information, no one has come forward yet with any clues. All that was left of the Jeep after police towed it away were two melted taillights, part of a melted tire, and a few other charred car parts spread over three spaces in the parking lot used by Heinz employees.

Six months after her death, police said they had exhausted all leads in the case. "There is no doubt that it was a murder," said Velma Goughler, a longtime friend of Stickle's and organizer of the campaign to raise funds for a private investigator. "There was hair in the door, blood was everywhere, her belongings thrown outside the vehicle. A trail of blood led from her apartment front door to the Jeep. Money, mace, and makeup were scattered near the vehicle. Someone intentionally set fire to the vehicle and burnt it down to its metal and killed her."

Officers also found blood outside her Jeep and on the door handle, leading investigators to initially believe she may have been beaten to death. But the coroner's office said the fire killed her. Investigators also said they doubt anyone could have injured her outside the Jeep and then placed her body upright in the seat, because she was a heavy woman. Jamie also had recently gone through a painful breakup with a longtime live-in girlfriend that week. According to Assistant Police Chief William Mullen, they looked at every potential suspect, anybody who could have had a reason to harm her. "We've interviewed thirty or forty people, traced her whereabouts that night, and consulted with experts. But we can't find anyone or anything that can explain what caused the Jeep to catch fire."

Several insurance industry experts on car fires have looked at the case but have not been able to come up with a reasonable answer either. "We're told the fire could not have started inside the cab, with a dropped cigarette or something," Mullen said. "But we have not found anything wrong with the Jeep that may have started it." Allegheny County Coroner Dr. Cyril Wecht said last year that Stickle's case is among a very few his office has handled where it can determine how a person died but not why.

Her friends can't think of anyone who would want to hurt Jamie. She was always helping people and actively raised awareness and money for breast cancer, AIDS, and multiple sclerosis. "There wasn't a cause Jamie Stickle wouldn't raise money for." After her death, members of the gay, lesbian, and bisexual community raised money for a reward. Jamie was openly gay, but police don't believe she was targeted because of her sexual orientation.

People who knew her said there was nothing she wouldn't do for a good cause. When she worked at Images, a downtown bar, she would cut hearts from construction paper in February for Valentine's Day and sell them to customers for a dollar apiece and donate the money to AIDS. In March, she would peddle shamrocks with ribbons and pins for St. Patrick's Day. She even allowed herself to be nominated to take part in an ugly bartender contest to raise money. David Morrow said Stickle had worked for him for about two years. Once, he recalled she put together a benefit to raise money for a customer who died of a heart attack at age twenty-eight. His family had no money, and her efforts enabled them to pay for a funeral and headstone.

So why, friends and family want to know, why would someone want to set ablaze a thirty-three-year-old woman who helped raise thousands of dollars for charity? Margie Walls, Jamie's mother, continues to wait by the phone in her home in Uniontown, Fayette County, for some concrete answer regarding her daughter's death. "She wasn't just my daughter; she was my best friend," Walls said with a twinge of anger in her voice. "I don't get any answers when I ask what happened to her. I don't understand why someone can't tell me why this happened."

"It's horrible not knowing, just horrible," said David Morrow. "I think about it every day. Somebody must know or have seen what happened." Chuck Honse, Stickle's friend and former boss at Images nightclub, said he and others who helped organize the United for Jamie Campaign now must decide what to do with the $18,000 raised to reward the person who could identify someone who may have harmed Stickle. "We can't advertise it as a reward because they've never officially called it a crime," Honse said. "We're going to meet with the Lambda Foundation soon to decide what parameters will be placed on the money if it's used for her favorite charities."

"I'd hoped it was just a horrible accident," said Maria Warhola. Warhola, with her husband George, owns Warhola Recycling, the business that occupies the first floor of the building where Jamie lived in an upstairs apartment. "This girl was like our daughter. She was very happy here," Warhola said, adding that Stickle lived alone in the apartment with her Shih Tzu, and the victim worked several jobs, including cleaning the Warholas' north side home.

To date, no one has stepped forward with information to solve her murder.

Police still ask for your help with the unsolved murder of Jamie Stickle. They have said not to discount the relevance of any information you may know. Your piece of information may have a significant impact on the investigation when viewed in the context of what they already know. For further information, call the Pittsburgh police hotline at (412) 255-8477, or you can E-mail whokilled@rooftoppublishing.com, and we will pass along this information.

Research and development for this story was made possible by the assistance of the Pittsburgh Public Library, *Pittsburgh Post* and *Tribune-Review* newspapers, Pittsburgh police, and the friends and family of Jamie.

Who Killed Raymond Marzoch?

Forty-seven-year-old prison guard Raymond Marzoch, pictured to the left, knew how dangerous his job at the state penitentiary could be. Each day he entered the prison, there existed the possibility of himself or one of his comrades being assaulted, taken hostage by inmates, and even killed. It's a part of the job description all guards accept and understand in this very high-risk line of work. For Marzoch, this was his chosen career, having completed a bachelor's degree in administrative justice from the University of Pittsburgh.

Ray had considered the fact that his path could one day cross with current inmate family members and/or former prisoners in his day-to-day life outside of the penitentiary. Those types of concerns were not included in conversations he had with friends and associates; in fact, Ray's thoughts and comments to friends on being murdered were closer to home: "If I ever turn up dead, my wife killed me."

On February 15, 1986, Raymond Marzoch, husband and father of three young children, was found dead in his parked car inside the downtown Kauffman parking garage. Cause of death? One bullet fired into his right temple at close range. Ray had told friends and family he was meeting his wife, Diana, inside the Kauffman parking garage so they could eat a late lunch together. Other reports also suggest he was to meet another woman sometime later. Witnesses who heard the shot told police a woman was sitting in the back seat of Marzoch's yellow 1976 Plymouth Arrow shortly before a passerby found his body and alerted a security guard. Ray's .38-caliber handgun wasn't in the glove compartment, which police found open. An attorney found Marzoch's wallet the next day on top of a guardrail outside of One Oxford Center in downtown Pittsburgh.

Police always felt his wife was somehow involved in her husband's murder but could never get that one piece of solid proof to charge her. They even had an eyewitness to the shooting, Anne Sonkin, who claims she saw a woman and Marzoch sitting in his car the day of the shooting in the parking garage. Sonkin said the woman matched the description of Raymond's wife, but Sonkin could not pick her out of a lineup. Even the fact that the Marzochs had divorced in 1982 and remarried a year later was suspicious in itself. It just wasn't enough.

There also were the statements from two fellow correctional officers who claimed Ray told them he woke up on the couch from a nap one day and found his wife standing over him with a knife to his throat. Mr. Marzoch told other co-workers that his marriage was troubled, that he suspected his wife was seeing other men, and that he was afraid of her physically harming him.

The murder soon fell into the cold-case files and remained there for approximately twenty years. One day in 2005, then-deputy Pittsburgh police chief William Mullen walked into the homicide squad room. "Marzoch," he told two cold-case detectives, J.R. Smith and Scott Evans, "work on it." And they did. Focusing on the one suspect at the time, police and prosecutors felt they had enough to go to the Allegheny County investigative grand jury and present a case for murder against Ray's former wife for his death. Since Ray's unsolved murder in 1986, Diana had remarried and moved on with her life as Mrs. Diana Rader.

According to police and newspaper accounts, it was found that much of the information the grand jury reviewed was the same evidence police had had for twenty years. But detectives and prosecutors decided this grand jury, which has special powers to compel cooperation and obtain documents, was the best way to proceed. In re-examining old witnesses and questioning a few new ones, the grand jury pointed to various pieces of evidence incriminating Mrs. (Marzoch) Rader. One witness, Anna Wojzynski, provided police with the description of a woman she saw sitting in the car with Mr. Marzoch that afternoon. The witness said the man seemed happy but the woman was "pouting."

Police put together a photo array of women in 2005 who resembled the description and included both Diane and her daughter, Tari Epolito, then twenty-four, who looked very much like her mother did at the time of the murder back in 1986. Mrs. Wojzynski picked those two as the ones who most closely looked like the woman in the car. She chose the same two again in two other instances.

The grand jury also focused on various inconsistencies in statements. For example, Diane told detectives that she and her former husband (whom she divorced in 1982 and remarried a year later) got along well, while his co-workers said the opposite. The grand jury questioned her alibi, too. On the afternoon of the murder, she told detectives, she was at Spa Lady in the Olympia Shopping Center, where she took her ten-year-old son Jon for a haircut, went to lunch and then to Kmart with him, and returned home at about 5 p.m. But Officer Marzoch's co-workers said he told them they had planned to meet at Kaufmann's after his shift and then go to dinner.

The grand jury said there is "no corroborative evidence" that she was at the shopping center or with her son between 2 and 3 p.m., when her husband was killed.

Grand jurors noted other evidence or suspicious behavior pointing to her. For example, she collected $34,510 in life insurance benefits after his death. She and her three children also had a separate viewing at the funeral home after which she made arrangements for her husband to be cremated but never picked up the ashes. It was Mr. Marzoch's brother, Jerome, who then arranged for proper burial services. Also, according to the evidence, when Detectives Smith and Evans interviewed Diane last year, she denied ever owning a handgun. But the grand jury was provided with a purchase document indicating she bought a .22-caliber gun in 1974 and heard testimony from a cousin that she carried a gun in her purse.

The gun used in the slaying, however, was a .38 that belonged to Mr. Marzoch and which he kept in his glove box. Detectives never located the gun, but they did recover the slug that passed through Mr. Marzoch's head and through the driver's side window of the car.

In conclusion, the grand jurors acknowledged problems with "discrepancies and inconsistencies" in witness testimony and the "inevitable memory lapses" in recalling events from twenty years ago. Nevertheless, the grand jury was satisfied in the totality of the testimony and supporting physical evidence. Stating the evidence points to her as the killer of Raymond Marzoch, she clearly had both a motive and the opportunity to commit this crime. And her conduct, at or near the time of his death, painted a portrait of hostility toward him.

Results of the Allegheny County investigative grand jury resulted in the arrest of Diana Marzoch Rader, pictured to the left, on March 7, 2007, for the 1986 murder of her former husband, Raymond Marzoch. Diane, now sixty-two years old, was held in jail with no bond until a preliminary hearing that would occur in April. Ray's brother told the *Tribune-Review* newspaper, "We're so relieved that some sort of justice is finally coming about. My brother was my only sibling and he was a good hard-working man who didn't deserve to die that way. We've been waiting for this day for two decades."

In April 2007, prosecutors displayed their evidence in a three-day hearing before Common Pleas Judge Lawrence J. O'Toole in hopes the judge would conclude there was enough evidence to go to trial. During the hearing, witnesses testified that Ray felt his wife was going to kill him. Just two days before he was shot to death, he confided in William Miller, fifty-nine, who testified at the preliminary hearing that Marzoch was giving him a ride to the State Correctional Institution in Pittsburgh, where they both worked. When the two men stopped at a red light, Mr. Marzoch made the statement about his wife: "If I turn up dead, my wife killed me."

Mrs. Rader reportedly sat handcuffed at the defense table for the entire proceedings and showed no reaction as Mr. Miller recalled the conversation he had with her late husband or when the witness testified that Mr. Marzoch told him on another occasion that he'd awoken from a nap to find his wife standing over him with a knife. Miller said he did not know Mrs. Rader and had no reason to lie. A second jail guard, Raymond J. Kotomski, testified he'd heard Mr. Marzoch talk about waking up from a nap on the couch to see his wife standing over him with "a knife to his throat."

Prosecutor Daniel Fitzsimmons called a witness who had seen a couple in the Kaufmann's parking garage shortly before the shooting. Police believe that the defendant shot her husband in the car. This witness, Anne Sonkin, testified that she could not identify the woman in the parking lot, but she picked Mrs. Rader and her daughter out of a photo array and an in-person lineup.

At the conclusion of the hearings, Judge O'Toole ruled that there was not sufficient evidence to show Diana had committed the murder and dismissed all charges against her. She was free to go.

Police still ask for your help with this unsolved murder of Raymond Marzoch. They have said not to discount the relevance of any information you may know. Your piece of information may have a significant impact on the investigation when viewed in the context of what they already know. For further information, call Pittsburgh police at (412) 255-8477, or you can E-mail whokilled@rooftoppublishing.com, and we will pass along this information.

Research and development for this story was made possible by the assistance of the Pittsburgh Public Library, *Pittsburgh Post* and *Tribune-Review* newspapers, Pittsburgh police, and the friends and family of Raymond.

Who Killed Sandra Baker?

Sandra vanished on May 25, 2000, from Mercer County, Pennsylvania. At forty-six years old and after six marriages, she appeared on the surface to be on top of the world. Engaged to Billy Crea, a successful electrician, the two were in the midst of creating the perfect picturesque covered-bridge wedding. Then for no apparent reason, she disappeared without a trace. Billy told police he last saw Ms. Baker between 8:30 and 9 a.m. on May 25, 2000, at the Sheetz store in Pymatuning. Surveillance tapes at the store showed she left alone in her own vehicle, so the intensity to find her lessened some. Feelings were she had just gotten cold feet and took off. Police would later classify Ms. Baker's case as an abduction and homicide, though her body has never been found.

From this point on, her vanishing from the face of the earth has turned into one of the most bizarre police investigations in Pennsylvania's history. In the beginning, police theorized Sandra wasn't the victim of foul play, so they were somewhat relaxed on issuing missing person's bulletins or lookouts for her car. As it turned out, the car was repossessed two days after she vanished. Repo men followed their instructions and took the car away, unaware its driver might have been kidnapped and killed.

The car, which might have contained fibers, blood, or other evidence, was sold at an auction. State police did not discover the car's whereabouts until 2004, too late for it to be of value in the investigation. By then, the vehicle was "a pile of rubbish" in a salvage yard. Retired State Trooper Robert Lewis said he regrets his failure to secure the car when the investigation was in its infancy. He acknowledges making a colossal error, which might have helped conceal damning physical evidence. "It got right by me," he said. "I admit it. I had no idea where her car was."

As the case began to unfold, police found there was more to Sandra Baker and Billy Crea than they first thought. Baker was still married to a man in Florida, and Crea had two failed marriages himself and actually met Sandra in 1999 while separated from his second wife. And at least one of his ex-wives claimed he was a violent man. The second Mrs. Crea said in a police report that he had beaten and abducted her at gunpoint on October 31, 1997, in Austintown, Ohio, when he showed up at his estranged wife's home in violation of a restraining order.

With this new piece of the puzzle, troopers felt there was a motive to a possible homicide. Just as quickly as the case grew hot, it fizzled out again. Deborah Crea gave Austintown police two dramatically different stories of her encounter with her husband. First she said Billy had not been armed, had not hurt her, and had not forced her to go with him. Then she made a second statement, saying the first was a lie. "My reason for not telling the truth at first was pure fear that Billy would come back and kill me," she wrote in a statement to police on November 14, 1997.

That case ended in August 1998 with Billy being convicted of a misdemeanor for violating the restraining order. A common pleas judge in Mahoning County, Ohio, sentenced him to two years' probation.

After learning this information, the state police zeroed in on Billy Crea about what really happened to Ms. Baker, but they had no body and no physical evidence. He hired a lawyer and stopped talking to police and went on with his life. That wasn't good enough for Sandra's best friend, Linda Henry. She wasn't about to let the case go cold. Mrs. Henry, fifty-three, has been the one constant figure in the saga of the Baker case. She wrote politicians and network television producers when the investigation seemed stuck in quicksand. She regularly called police to share information. She even persuaded a dairy to put Sandra Baker's picture on its milk cartons, hoping the attendant publicity would help crack the case. A self-employed house cleaner in Greenville, Mrs. Henry never expected to spend her life crusading to have a murder case prosecuted. Then again, she never expected somebody she loved to be abducted. Eventually, the investigation did fall into the cold-case files. Or so everyone thought.

Known to only a few people, Billy had hired Private Investigator Clifford Aley, who was also his best friend, to conduct a financial background check on Sandra before the wedding. The private investigator learned she was deeply in debt and still married to a man in Florida. According to Clifford, Billy then switched his direction for the investigator and asked his friend to look into her disappearance.

What occurs next could go down in the national private investigators hall of fame and make true crime annals of history.

Tragically, it took the police detectives' focus off finding Sandra Baker and directed it to PI Clifford Aley. Instead of continuing their investigation into a possible murder, police and Mercer County prosecutors focused their attention on Clifford and charged him with four felonies, all for hindering the investigation of what happened to Sandra. Out of the blue, he told police and prosecutors that Billy had killed Sandra. "He said William Crea confessed to him that he murdered his fiancée," said Assistant District Attorney Tim Bonner, lead prosecutor in the Baker case.

The problem with Clifford's allegations against his friend was that he lied to police and failed polygraph questions that led detectives to believe he actually was involved in Sandra's disappearance. In the court affidavit seeking an arrest warrant for Mr. Aley, state police branded Billy Crea the suspect in Ms. Baker's disappearance and presumed killing. The news media then questioned Billy Crea about the arrest of his private investigator. "He doesn't have any comment," said Mr. Crea's attorney, James Ecker of Pittsburgh. "I know nothing. He knows nothing."

As the noose around Clifford Aley's own neck began to tighten, his lips seemed to loosen up against his former friend. Clifford began confessing details he allegedly knew about the disappearance of Sandra Baker. While doing so, he admitted to being involved in helping Billy cover up facts about the case that would forever impede the police from possibly solving her now-apparent murder. Clifford admitted he actually called the finance company that was looking for Sandra's car for non-payment. In fact, he directed the repo truck driver to the location of her car. Even with this new turn of events, no arrests in connection with Sandra's alleged homicide took place. Billy Crea's attorney was now even more steadfast. Attorney James Ecker said he was reluctant to talk about an ongoing trial involving somebody else. "I have no comment other than Mr. Crea is still where he was when this began, charged with nothing and innocent until proven guilty."

Five years later, on January 11, 2006, Clifford went on trial for the felony charges of providing false information to police and for hindering their investigation. During trial, the Mercer County prosecutor's contention was, "He gave information that turned out to be significant lies that hindered this investigation and apprehension of the killer," repeatedly lying to state police about the disappearance and presumed death of Sandra Kay Baker. District Attorney Tim Bonner stated in his opening statement to the jury, "During four years of deceit, Mr. Aley misled police and blocked them from finding clues that would have solved the mystery of Ms. Baker's slaying."

According to newspaper accounts of the trial, Clifford came to court each day in a wheelchair. Pale, heavy, and looking older than his forty-eight years, he sought out reporters and told them his health was being ruined because of inhumane conditions in the Mercer County Jail. He had been held there since his arrest in July 2005. Clifford took notes while the prosecution played a tape of his first interview with police on June 18, 2000. Mr. Bonner said the former private investigator had begun his string of lies that day. In the recording, Clifford said he did not know Sandra and had never investigated her. He even denied knowing that his close friend Billy Crea was engaged to her.

The jury learned that under pressure from police four years later, Clifford finally changed his story. He admitted Billy had hired him to do an investigation on Sandra in 2000. He found that she had been married six times and was still married to a Florida man when she became engaged to his friend. Clifford then dropped his bombshell. He said Billy told him he had strangled her after an argument about infidelity. Clifford said Billy put her body in some sort of container and hid it in Mercer County.

The prosecutor also used Mr. Aley's own words to suggest that her slaying was premeditated, not the result of an argument. Clifford told police that Billy asked him on May 24, 2000, to dispose of Sandra Baker's car the day before she disappeared. Knowing she was behind on her car payments, Clifford called the finance company and said he would supply information to help it repossess her vehicle. On May 25, the very day Sandra vanished, he called the company again. Mr. Aley said her blue 1988 Honda Accord was parked at the Shenango Valley Mall. Repo men hauled away her Honda and any evidence it contained. Police did not find Ms. Baker's car until 2004. By then, it sat in a scrap yard, crushed.

In one of his taped statements, Clifford admitted to owning a blue 1988 Honda Accord that looked like Baker's. He said he bought the car the spring she disappeared. The prosecutors' implication to the jury was the car gave Clifford a ready explanation if anybody claimed he had been seen driving Sandra's Honda. Clifford said he remembered that the last statement Billy made to the police was saying he heard from his fiancée in a frantic phone call the afternoon she vanished. Allegedly she told him she was in danger but hoped to return home in a couple of days. Clifford admitted Billy said that was all a lie and part of his plan to throw the cops off of him. When asked by the prosecution and police why he had lied for all of those years, Clifford said he feared Billy would harm him and his children if he cooperated with investigators.

After being found guilty, the judge sentenced him to eighteen to forty-eight months for hindering the state investigation into the disappearance and presumed death of Sandra Kay Baker. In one last twist to this story, later in September 2006, Common Pleas Judge Francis Fornelli sentenced him to an additional four to twelve months in a state prison for threatening guards, lawyers, and judges while he was housed at the Mercer County Jail in November.

When asked why he made the threats against everyone, forty-nine-year-old Clifford said he was sitting in jail awaiting his trial for obstruction, when anger consumed him. He said he was frustrated because he was behind bars and Billy Crea remained free. Then he said he remembered how Billy had threatened to kill his children if he cooperated with police in the Baker case. But instead of telling his lawyer or asking police to make sure his family was safe, Clifford threatened to maim the guards, shoot everyone in the courtroom where his case was being heard, and blow up the county building.

"What you did was illogical," Judge Fornelli told him. "You say Crea threatened your children, so then you threatened other people." The judge said Mr. Aley, who stands six feet six inches tall and weighed 360 pounds when he made the threats, caused fear among guards who had to escort him to court.

No one has ever been charged with the disappearance and presumed murder of Sandra Kay Baker. The police and prosecutor have called Billy Crea the killer, but he has yet to be arrested for her death. The only conviction in this case is against former private investigator Clifford Aley for impeding the murder investigation. Technically, this is still an unsolved murder investigation.

Police still ask for your help with this unsolved murder of Sandra Baker. They have said not to discount the relevance of any information you may know. Your piece of information may have a significant impact on the investigation when viewed in the context of what they already know. For further information, call the Mercer County Sheriff's Department at (724) 962-5711, or you can E-mail whokilled@rooftoppublishing.com, and we will pass along this information.

Research and development for this story was made possible by the assistance of the Pittsburgh Public Library, *Pittsburgh Post* and *Tribune-Review* newspapers, Mercer County police, and the friends and family of Sandra.

Who Killed 16-year-old Raquel Tilisha Carter?

O f the unsolved murders in 2001 the most baffling to police is the case of Raquel Tilisha Carter, a sixteen-year-old whose body was found April 29 in a clearing in Homewood. Willis Humphrey of Banfield Street said he and his nephew Ronald Garrett found the body in a clearing about twenty yards from his front door after his dog kept trotting back and forth from the body to the driveway. Police have found little information about her activities or companions in the hours before her body was discovered around 11 a.m. at the end of Banfield Street. Although there was little blood, police said they believe she was stabbed at the site and left to die.

Raquel's mother, Chris Carter Brown, said she last saw her daughter around 7 p.m. April 28 at the home of her own mother, Shirley Carter, on Frankstown Avenue in Homewood. Brown and her boyfriend, Loren Clemm, were invited to a dinner party and dropped off Brown's son at the Homewood house. Raquel was there.

"We just saw a shadow of her," Clemm said, remembering Raquel's silhouette in the doorway. He said they went to the dinner party and returned to the Frankstown Avenue home around 2:30 a.m. to pick up eleven-year-old Jerell, Brown's son. When he got in the car to go home, Brown's son remarked, "Mom, Raquel's not home yet."

"I didn't think anything about it," Brown recalled. She said Raquel's plan for the evening was to stay with her grandmother, and Brown said she assumed her daughter had slipped in and gone to bed without Jerell noticing. The next day, Clemm saw a television news story about the discovery of an unidentified woman. It mentioned she wore three distinctive rings. He said he did not make a connection until Brown's grandmother, who also lived in Homewood with Shirley Carter, called and said the woman must be Raquel. "We all knew she wore those rings," Brown said.

Later, they learned from Jerell that Raquel had left her grandmother's house between 9 and 9:30 p.m. They think she may have gone to the playground across the street to talk to her friends. Brown said they later heard from police that Raquel may have gotten into a red car with someone she knew. "But she didn't intend to go anywhere," Clemm said. "She wouldn't have left without her purse." In the purse was an address book, and police have called all the friends in the book and found nothing, Brown said.

Major Crimes Commander Maurita Bryant said police have hit a wall in the crime. "We're starting to re-interview people we've already interviewed." Most of Raquel's friends described her as a friendly, happy girl who earned good grades. Bryant said police have even checked out a rumor that a group of girls did not like her and was planning to do her harm, but nothing has come of it. But Bryant said no suspects have been eliminated. "Nothing is ruled out until we catch somebody," she said.

When police arrived, it appeared that Carter's body was lying near or on the Penn Hills-Pittsburgh border. The investigation fell to the city after city surveyors determined that the body was on the city side of the boundary, said county Homicide Sergeant Tom Glenn. Although there was little blood where the girl lay, city Police Lieutenant Thomas Stangrecki said police believe she was stabbed at the site and left to die. According to Commander Bryant, the last time anyone had seen Carter was about 9:30 that Saturday night when she visited her maternal grandmother's home on Frankstown Avenue in Homewood.

Hope Henry, an academic counselor at Woodland Hills High School, said Carter lived with her paternal grandmother while attending high school for tenth and most of eleventh grades. Henry said Carter, an above-average student, was doing well but left in March to go to her father in North Carolina. The tall attractive teen returned to Pittsburgh on April 9 and enrolled at Allderdice High School. High school friends and neighbors on Wilner Drive said they last saw Carter Friday when she rode the bus home. They said she was a happy, outgoing girl who visited her maternal grandmother in Homewood every Friday.

"She liked to talk a lot and laugh a lot and smile a lot," said fourteen-year-old Dorian Brentley. Brentley lives a few doors from Carter's mother, Chris Brown, her two sisters and brother. Carter was the oldest child in the family. Chermer McCain and Lashelle Mays, both sixteen and juniors at Allderdice, said they latched on to Carter after meeting in a math class about three weeks prior. They said she told them she had just returned from North Carolina. "She used to be with us all the time. Before she came, it was us two," McCain said. "Then when she came, it was us three. Now it's just us two again."

Loren Clemm, Chris Brown's boyfriend, said the family declined comment.

Police still ask for your help with this unsolved murder of Raquel Carter. They have said not to discount the relevance of any information you may know. Your piece of information may have a significant impact on the investigation when viewed in the context of what they already know. For further information, call Pittsburgh police at (412) 255-8477, or you can E-mail whokilled@rooftoppublishing.com, and we will pass along this information.

Research and development for this story was made possible by the assistance of the Pittsburgh Public Library, *Pittsburgh Post* and *Tribune-Review* newspapers, Pittsburgh police, and the friends and family of Raquel Carter.

Who Killed My Sons?

This was a question posed on the billboard, pictured to the left, located near the intersection of Frankstown Avenue at Wilkinsburg until July 2001. After that, Wanda Broadus was unable to pay the $350 fee any longer. She thanked the people at Lamar's sign company for allowing her an extra thirty days more exposure in hopes someone would come forward and solve the murders of her two sons, Scott and George, who were brutally murdered seven years apart. Mrs. Broadus prayed her determination would unearth new leads in the murders of two of her children.

"Maybe the sign will jog the memory of someone who knows what happened." The billboard gave the two men's names and years of death and underneath said, "Please report any information to the police." Wanda moved to Florida some thirteen years ago, saying at the time she still lived with the void in her heart of the loss of her two boys. Not knowing who to blame just made it worse. Scott and George White were murdered in separate incidents. Nineteen-year-old Scott was stabbed to death on May 7, 1983, after three men demanded money. His older brother, twenty-seven-year-old George, was shot in 1990 during a drug deal that turned sour, according to Broadus's husband, Dalton.

Scott White had only been out of Peabody High School one year when he was killed at about 3:30 a.m. Initially, police reported that Scott was killed as he was returning home from his dishwashing job at a Baum Boulevard diner. According to Dalton Broadus, Scott and a friend were actually walking home from a party. Three men in a car pulled up next to Scott while he was walking on East Liberty Boulevard near Negley Run Boulevard in East Liberty. His friend had already crossed the street and was waiting for him on the other side.

The men, who had been at the same party, got out of the car and demanded money. White refused to give it to them. When they rushed him, he tried to fight, but one of the men stabbed him in the heart. He died at the scene. Ultimately, Wanda Broadus said the men fled without taking Scott's money. "His wallet was still there," she said. It still contained the picture of his girlfriend, a few cards, and about $25. No arrests were ever made in the killing, according to Wanda.

In George's murder, there seemed to be a break on June 22, 1993, when William Washington was arrested for his murder. Noel Lawrence Wilson, then twenty-one, said he and White had been walking on Larimer Avenue at about 2:30 a.m. on June 5, 1990, when the shooting occurred. Wilson said Washington stopped his car and asked to buy cocaine from White. But when

White and Wilson got into the car, Washington pulled a .357 Magnum and tried to rob them.

A struggle for the gun ensued. A couple of rounds were fired in the car, but White and Wilson managed to jump out. They ran in opposite directions, but Washington shot at them and a bullet caught White in the back, severing his spinal cord. He died eleven days later in UPMC Presbyterian. During a coroner's inquest on July 1, 1993, Wilson was unable to identify Washington. The case was thrown out on March 17, 1994. "It's very empty still. I'd like to see something done," Mrs. Broadus told a *Pittsburgh Post* reporter in 2003 from her St. Petersburg home. "Justice. I just want justice."

Police still ask for your help with the unsolved murders of Scott and George White. They have said not to discount the relevance of any information you may know. Your piece of information may have a significant impact on the investigation when viewed in the context of what they already know. For further information, call the Pittsburgh police at (412) 255-8477, or you can E-mail whokilled@rooftoppublishing.com, and we will pass along this information.

Research and development for this story was made possible by the assistance of the Pittsburgh Public Library, *Pittsburgh Post* and *Tribune-Review* newspapers, local police, and the friends and family of the Whites and Broaduses.

Who Killed Robert Kart?

Robert Kart was a hardworking and good man, a loving husband, and a good father. Then why would the police arrest his son Herbert for trying to hire a hit man to kill his dad? And when the first offer to hire a professional killer fell through, did the son try again until someone actually took the contract?

It was a hot, clear night on June 29, 1989, and Robert Kart was working late again. At sixty-three, he still put in a full day and then some. At 8 p.m., he called his wife, Sella, to say he'd be home within an hour. She waited. Nine o'clock came and went, but her husband didn't arrive. She called him at their business, the Slush Puppie distributorship on McCague Street in Swissvale. No answer. The clock ticked away.

"The day of the murder, I was frantic because my husband didn't come home," Sella Kart, sixty-nine, said in an interview. "I called around. I called the hospitals. I called and called and called and called, and I couldn't get any response." Finally, at 10:45 p.m., she grew tired of waiting. She called the police.

They found Robert Kart beaten to death in his store, a 500-pound ice cream freezer on top of him and not a shred of hard evidence to point to his killer. He was a successful businessman who had been a fixture in the neighborhood for years, a loving grandfather, and a hardworking father of two sons.

It appeared that robbery was the motive. Whoever did it ransacked the office, breaking open two desk drawers where cash was kept, and left the garage door open. But strangely, Kart was left face down in a pool of blood still wearing a gold bracelet, gold necklace, watch, and his wedding band. Kart's killer still has not been found. Pathologists determined Kart died from blunt force trauma to the head, but investigators never retrieved a murder weapon. There were no witnesses, and no one has been arrested. Allegheny County Police have not given up hope of solving it.

They are still actively working on the case and explained it's not put away in a cupboard to never be worked on. It's assigned to a detective who has an active interest in it. They are periodically making attempts to see if they can unearth some new information. Kart's widow lacks confidence in the investigation. She believes the investigation was compromised from the start by Swissvale police, whom she claims allowed the crime scene to be contaminated by patrons from the M&M Lounge nearby. And she blamed county detectives for wasting precious time scrutinizing her family in a search for suspects.

As a result, she believes her husband's killer will never be caught. "I feel that the murder will never be solved if it hasn't been solved by now, and I don't see any purpose to my bringing up everything," said Sella Kart in a June 1999 interview with *Pittsburgh Post*. "I'm very bitter because they went after the family instead of going to the real perpetrator, and he fell through the cracks, whoever it may be." Although Officer Brennan, who found Sella's husband, said he did not recall Kart being pinned under an ice cream freezer, Sella Kart said the lone Swissvale patrolman who found her husband summoned the "barflies" at the M&M to help him lift the freezer. In doing so, she said evidence was destroyed and the crime scene was contaminated—something she claims a retired county detective told her the next day. Brennan said he had never heard that the crime scene was not properly preserved, but acknowledged it was possible. Then-Swissvale police chief James Ohrman declined comment.

Robert and Sella Kart had built their business from the ground up. Both Squirrel Hill natives, they met on a blind date and married a few years later. He was a World War II veteran, a master sergeant in the army who served under General George S. Patton. Robert Kart's father owned the Triangle Candy and Tobacco Company, and he worked there before heading off on his own in 1973. At a candy convention in Las Vegas, Sella Kart had a headache and bought an orange Slush Puppie from a vendor, swallowed an aspirin along with it, and noticed a sign saying that franchises were available.

She showed it to her husband. By the time he died, their business had moved from Shadyside to Swissvale and expanded by leaps and bounds. Slush Puppie of Pittsburgh Inc. sold equipment to customers in thirteen counties at more than 500 separate locations. In the little spare time he had, Robert Kart volunteered for organizations that helped handicapped people and was on the board of Allegheny East Mental Health and Mental Retardation Center in Penn Hills, Sella Kart said. The Karts' younger son, Steve, is himself handicapped.

"Bob did a lot of good in his life. He was very well-liked," she said.

In the investigative frenzy that followed the murder, detectives drew up a list of current and former employees, looking for someone who might have wanted to harm Kart. They administered polygraph tests. They took hair samples from Sella Kart and her eldest son, Herbert. All the attention made Sella Kart so angry that she sought a restraining order against a particular county detective whose dogged inquiries she interpreted as harassment. In January 1992, police thought they had a break in the case. They arrested Herbert Kart and accused him of hiring a hit man in April 1989 to kill his father.

At that point, Herbert Kart was going through tough times. His marital life was in turmoil; he also had gone bankrupt in 1988, the year before his father's murder. Things became tenser when his father fired him from Slush Puppie after he had worked there for thirteen years. A police affidavit filed to support the arrest warrant accused Herbert Kart of offering a man named Eric Miller $5,000 up front and $5,000 afterward to beat his father to death and make it look like a robbery. Miller, who was also interviewed by the *Post*, said he met Herbert Kart while working at a Squirrel Hill shoe store, but he declined to discuss the case any further.

Another *Post* story, published on January 14, 1992, about the alleged hit to kill his father reads as follows:

> A Squirrel Hill man was arrested today on charges of trying to hire someone to kill his father in April 1989. Although police said Herbert Kart, 39 of Beechwood Boulevard was not successful in hiring a hit man at that time his father was murdered three months later. The murder of Robert Kart, 63 of Churchill, has not been solved, and his son has not been charged in the killing. The elder Kart was struck over the head

and killed on June 29, 1989, during an apparent robbery of his store.

According to police, Miller rejected Herbert Kart's request. In February 1992, the Allegheny County district attorney's office withdrew the solicitation of murder charge against Herbert Kart. Police still suspect Herbert was somehow involved in arranging his father's death, even though Sella Kart is adamant her son was framed. Herbert Kart's attorney also insists his client had nothing to do with his father's death and went on record with the following statement.

"Herb Kart is innocent of this crime, has always been innocent of this crime." At that time, ten years had passed. "Let him live his life," said David Shrager, a Pittsburgh lawyer who represented Herbert in 1992. Herbert Kart allegedly works at an auto dealership in Monroeville, and court records indicate times have not gotten much easier for him since his father's death. In 1990, his ex-wife obtained a protection from abuse order against him. According to court records, he was accused of breaking into her home with a sledgehammer. Another protection from abuse order was granted in 1996, and the couple's divorce was finalized in 1998.

In 1997, Herbert Kart was arrested in Homestead and charged with burglary and criminal mischief. Police accused him of breaking into a woman's home and stealing her thirty-one-inch color television set. The woman did not show up for the hearing, and the charges were withdrawn. For Sella Kart, life has gone on, but it has been emptier without her husband. She had managed to reopen their store after his death and ran it until July 1997, when she sold the business. But during those eight years, Sella Kart told the *Post* she could never bring herself to go to the spot where her husband's body was found.

Sella said she never healed and never will, and she mourns for her husband every day. Mrs. Kart described her husband as a hardworking, very wonderful husband, devoted to his family and to her. The county police will continue their quest for Robert Kart's killer.

Police still ask for your help with this unsolved murder of Robert Kart. They have said not to discount the relevance of any information you may know. Your piece of information may have a significant impact on the investigation when viewed in the context of what they already know. For further information, call Swissvale police at (412) 271-0430, or you can E-mail whokilled@rooftoppublishing.com, and we will pass along this information.

Research and development for this story was made possible by the assistance of the Pittsburgh Public Library, *Pittsburgh Post* and *Tribune-Review* newspapers, the Allegheny County Sheriff's Department, and the friends and family of Robert Kart.

Who Killed Jane Doe and Her Unborn Child?

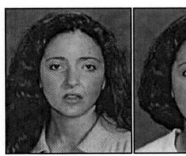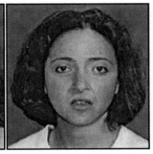

Thirty years ago and 260 miles away from Pittsburgh, a teenager walking along the banks of the Lehigh River outside this Luzerne County town in the Pocono Mountains made a gruesome discovery. On December 20, 1976, the dismembered remains of a young woman, pictured above, and her full-term female fetus were found. Police are no closer to finding the woman's killer because they are still missing one crucial bit of information—her name.

Try as they might, authorities haven't come close to making an identification. And their prospects dim a little more with each passing year. "Unfortunately, it's as cold as cold can be," said Corporal Thomas McAndrew, a state police detective who took over the case a year ago. "The killer's never been caught, and never will be until we find out who she is." The woman was strangled, shot, dismembered, and stuffed into three suitcases that were flung over a bridge along Interstate 80.

The killer was probably aiming for the Lehigh River 300 feet below but missed. Two of the suitcases broke open on impact, spilling the victim's head and torso and her female fetus. The third suitcase contained the woman's arms and legs. Her nose and ears had been cut off.

The coroner estimated she had been dead less than twenty-four hours. The crime scene yielded a wealth of evidence, but little of it was useful. In addition to her remains, investigators had the suitcases, all of them the same size and missing their handles. Some body parts were wrapped in a rust-colored chenille bedspread; six soggy sections of the *New York Sunday News* covered her torso. A series of letters and numbers, written in ink on the palm of her left hand, provided a tantalizing clue. But a police check of license plates and CB call signs turned up nothing.

"She haunts me, she really does," said Nancy Monahan, the Pennsylvania director of the Doe Network, a group of amateur sleuths that seeks to attach names to unidentified bodies. "I've had dreams about her." Dreams and questions, such as: How could a young woman, about to give birth, have simply vanished days or weeks before Christmas and no one reported her missing? Was she someone on the margins of society? An illegal immigrant perhaps? Was her own family covering up for the killer, and that's why no one came forward? And what about that writing on her hand?

At the White Haven Police Department where an artist's conception of what the victim looked like hangs on a wall, Patrolman Thomas Szoke has his own theories about the case. "My feeling is she is probably a runaway from another state and her family doesn't know what happened to her," he said.

"Or she may have been a throwaway, where the parent says, 'You're fifteen, get out.'" The victim's family might have even filed a missing person's report, Patrolman Szoke said, but such a report, if it exists, would likely be collecting dust in a police department file cabinet somewhere.

Corporal McAndrew said he would like to exhume the body to gather DNA samples, but the process is time-consuming and expensive. And while DNA samples can be run through FBI and missing person's databases, a match would be a long shot given the time elapsed. "DNA testing can be used in unidentified body cases, but it is not an important tool at this time because the number of people whose DNA is on record anywhere represents a very small percentage of the population," State Police Spokesman Jack Lewis said. The victim had previous dental work and her fetus was healthy at the time of death, indicating the woman took care of herself and her unborn daughter.

For Corporal McAndrew, learning her identity would be a small way to give her some dignity. "It's amazing that no one has identified her, that somebody out there isn't missing her," he said. The victim and her fetus are buried in a paupers' cemetery several miles from where the remains were found. The tomb is marked with a simple white cross and a small granite marker that says, "Beth Doe," which, unless there is a miraculous break in the case, is how history will remember her.

- **Estimated Age**: Her year of birth was estimated between 1954 and 1960.

- **Approximate Height and Weight**: 5'4", 163 cm; 150 lbs, 68 kg.

- **Distinguishing Characteristics**: Brown eyes, brown hair. She had a small circular mole above her left eye, a mole on her left cheek, and a 5.5" scar on her left leg, just above the heel. She had no previous fractures.

- **Dentals**: Available.

- **Medical Information**: She was carrying a full-term white female fetus. It is possible that the moles on her face developed at some time during her pregnancy.

Police still ask for your help with this unsolved murder of Jane Doe and her unborn daughter. They have said not to discount the relevance of any information you may know. Your piece of information may have a significant impact on the investigation when viewed in the context of what they already know. For further information, call the Pennsylvania State Police at (717) 783-5524, or you can E-mail whokilled@rooftoppublishing.com, and we will pass along this information.

Research and development for this story was made possible by the assistance of the Pittsburgh Public Library, *Pittsburgh Post* and *Tribune-Review* newspapers, and state, county, and city police.

Who Killed My Mother?

Carol Burkovac could stand on the Belle Vernon side of the Monongahela River and stare across the water into the town of Charleroi. A strange presence had been drawing her to the tiny Pennsylvania town for as long as she could remember. Being adopted as a baby into the Burkovac family left many unanswered questions regarding her natural parents. Carol's research began as she wanted to learn of her real family and how she had come to be adopted. In a quest to learn about her past, she would have to resurrect an all-but-forgotten unsolved murder from twenty-seven years ago.

Just as the sun was rising on June 11, 1980, a mineworker driving through the country to secure company outbuildings thought he was approaching a dead deer on the road. As the vehicle's headlights shined closer upon the mound in the middle of the road, John Harida slowed to a crawl and realized it was a body. "I hollered, 'Do you need help? Are you all right?'" said Harida, who was then a thirty-three-year-old employee of Mathies Mine company. There was no response. Harida was afraid to stop. He had a hunch he had stumbled upon a homicide scene and the killer might be hiding in the woods.

In the quiet stillness of that spring morning, he drove some distance to the next house along Patterson Road in Nottingham Township to summon state police. In no time, police crowded over the body of a woman with shoulder-length gray-streaked brown hair, wearing a blood-soaked imitation red leather jacket and checkered pantsuit. Police did not recognize the victim. During the autopsy at Washington Hospital, the medical examiner found seventeen stab wounds, some of them deep and long across the chest and torso of the woman who appeared to be in her fifties.

A strike from one of the killer's knife wounds pierced the heart to kill the stranger who appeared to have been in good health prior to death. The coroner also determined she had abrasions to both hands, indicating the woman attempted to fight off her attacker. No identification was found on the body with gray-green eyes, leading investigators to suspect robbery as a motive. But a door key was found safety-pinned to her trousers. Following brief newspaper accounts of the slaying, police received an anonymous telephone tip that the victim might be fifty-five-year-old North Charleroi widow Edna Mae Jarvis. Investigators went to her residence at 308 Sheppard Street, slid the key into the lock, and opened the door to her unkempt apartment.

A sister from nearby Fallowfield Township, Margaret Pennline, who was the county's director of personnel, later confirmed positive identification. Charleroi police took the lead in the investigation because Jarvis was last seen at Syl's Bar in a working-class neighborhood at the north edge of the borough. Police set up a roadblock, stopping cars to ask drivers if they had seen anything suspicious. It didn't help. A suspect never surfaced, said District Judge Larry Hopkins, a former Charleroi patrolman who was working the beat.

Little else appears to have been said publicly about the case until Carol Bukovac, who was adopted as a newborn, went in search of her birth parents about eight years ago.

As a newborn, she had been taken into the home of Charles and Thelma Bukovac of Belle Vernon, a town just across the Monongahela River from Charleroi. In an adoption arranged by the couple's physician, the baby girl would probably never know her natural birth family.

Bukovac was in her mid-forties when she decided it was time to learn more about her birth family using records her adoptive mother had filed away. Through a third party, telephone calls were placed to people living in Mon Valley listed under the last name of Gottheld, Jarvis's name by her first husband. In no time, news of the woman's murder was conveyed to Bukovac. "It was devastating," she said. Bukovac also learned of two half-sisters, one in Charleroi and another in Virginia, who were taken from Jarvis as children by child services because she "was dragging them off to bars." Other newfound relatives appeared hesitant to talk much about Jarvis, she said.

Carol has heard many rumors about her mother's homicide, including that the killer's identity was never much of a secret in town. Someone relayed another story to her that Jarvis had been driven away from Syl's Bar the night of the murder in a car with three younger men, one of whom was politically connected in the borough. What is known for sure is that Jarvis had been brutally beaten by three men and admitted to Mon Valley Hospital before her murder. Jarvis told a family member then that her attackers "would come back and kill her," Bukovac said, relaying what Jarvis had revealed to a daughter from her hospital bed.

Bukovac said she suspected citizens of Charleroi remained quiet about the murder because of her mother's reputation. Bukovac has since asked state police to take another look at the case. "I would just like to know. I just think that's a normal thing. If your mother was murdered, you want to know why." Police appear to be honoring her request, even though they are faced with a long list of unsolved homicide cases in the region.

Trooper Bev Ashton reviewed the Jarvis case and filed a new report with her commander, Lieutenant Rick Sethman. This was one murder that the cold-case homicide unit that formed in 1999 had yet to focus upon. Then just as slowly, it took Washington County record-keepers another two months to even find Jarvis's coroner's report after the *Observer-Reporter* requested it. In murder cases where people are tight-lipped about the victim, police with little evidence are strapped for clues. "Unfortunately, sometimes that will happen," Ashton said.

Police still ask for your help with this unsolved murder of Edna Mae Jarvis. They have said not to discount the relevance of any information you may know. Your piece of information may have a significant impact on the investigation when viewed in the context of what they already know. For further information, call Pennsylvania State Police at (717) 783-5524, or you can E-mail whokilled@rooftoppublishing.com, and we will pass along this information.

Research and development for this story was made possible by the assistance of the Washington County Public Library, the *Observer-Reporter* newspaper in Washington, Pennsylvania, and the Pennsylvania State Police, Washington County Sheriff's Department, and city police.

Who Wrote to Police Confessing to Murder?

In late June of 1996, Butler County law enforcement received a letter postmarked Pittsburgh from an unidentified person wanting to confess to three murders. Then-district attorney Tim McCune and Butler State Police Captain Terry Seilhamer held a news conference admitting they had the letter. "The prime motivation behind the letter appears to be feelings of remorse and a sincere desire to obtain help," McCune said. Seilhamer added that the author has "expressed a willingness to surrender to police." At the writer's urging, authorities held the news conference as a signal they're willing to help.

The district attorney urged the author of the letter to contact the Butler State Police or the DA's office. McCune promised if he turned himself in and cooperated with authorities, "I will see to it that he receives the proper evaluation from mental health professionals. Psychological and psychiatric treatment could then be made available to him … We feel the best thing for him to do is to turn himself in." At the time, McCune said the man indicated he did not want to hurt anyone else, but McCune added that authorities were treating the letter with "some sense of urgency." The man did not indicate how he could be reached but urged authorities to contact him through the media. That would be the last time anyone heard from the author of the letter.

Police admitted the letter did not list the names of the victims but contained enough specific references to locations and individuals to lead authorities to a short list of possible cases. The information he did provide appeared to match up to some of the cases they were investigating. The media was able to put together its own list of possible victims in the area of unsolved murders:

Alice M. Kellar, twenty-three, of Penn was murdered on December 13, 1965.

Dominick R. Peoples, twenty-five, of Ambridge was murdered on November 22, 1977.

Timothy E. Saloom, twenty-eight, of Mercer was murdered on February 8, 1991.

Vicki L. Sinz, twenty-two, of Butler was murdered on July 25, 1981.

Mary J. Stevenson, twenty-five, of Pittsburgh's North Side was murdered on June 4, 1988.

Mary M. Burke, thirty-one, of Penn Township was murdered on September 26, 1979.

Emily I. Johnson, thirty-six, of Clinton was murdered on June 11, 1990.

Researching each victim's case, we have found some information about their lives and murders.

Alice Kellar

After almost forty years of chasing leads and hitting dead ends, state police believed they would make an arrest in the strangulation death of twenty-three-year-old Alice Kellar, pictured below, who was found in her Penn Township, Butler County, bedroom by her husband, Karl, on the evening of December 13, 1965. Her sons, nineteen-month-old Karl Jr. who was in a playpen and six-month-old Harry who was in a crib, were unharmed.

For decades now, police have been unable to link evidence to the murderer. Kellar's parents have since died, and her sons are grown men. Her husband, Karl, still lived in the area in 2005 just off Route 8 in Middlesex Township, Butler County. The Kellar case might have been put on hold periodically throughout the years, but state police say they never abandoned it. Working against the passage of time, fading memories, and the changes from one investigator to the next, police still plugged away at the case. "Time's working against you," said Corporal Ray Melder, head of the State Police Criminal Investigation Assessment Unit in Butler County. "Witnesses die, and you end up with information you're not able to confirm it or deny it." Luckily, new information surfaced six months ago.

Police have a suspect, although Melder refused to publicly name the person he believes killed Kellar. "I feel confident I know who did this," he said. "In the near future, we will have it done."

Karl Kellar Sr. was more forthcoming. He said that he believes police have wrongly fingered him as the murderer. "I can't tell you a damn thing," said Kellar Sr. in a June 2005 interview with the *Tribune-Review*. "I can't tell you because, damn it, they have their opinion and I have mine."

Even after four decades, the death of the mother he never knew remains too difficult to discuss for Karl Kellar Jr. During a brief conversation, he said he couldn't bring himself to rehash the suffering but did state, "I would like to get the case solved. But it's been the same thing from police for years."

Alice Kellar's older brother Russ Lenhardt of Harrison momentarily allowed himself to open a vault of painful memories he would just prefer to remain locked, at least to the public. "It's been two years," he said at the time of the news article since he last heard from police about his sister's murder.

He and his sister were raised in Albion, a town of about 1,500 people in Erie County. Alice was a high school cheerleader. "She was just a bouncing, smiling, very active girl," Lenhardt said. Alice attended Edinboro State College, where she earned a degree in teaching. She taught special education at a Butler elementary school before marrying in 1962. Alice was last seen alive at about 7:30 a.m. on December 13, 1965.

Her husband was the director of the science department at Hampton Township Junior-Senior High School and head of the district's teachers association. He told his wife he would be late getting home as he hoped to finish some Christmas shopping. Police reports say when he arrived home, he found his wife on the bedroom floor with three of his neckties knotted around her throat. She wore only sneakers. Her jaw was dislocated; her nose was bloodied. A nearby table was overturned and broken. Nothing was taken from the house. An autopsy indicated Alice had been dead between six and twelve hours before she was found. There was no evidence of sexual assault.

Hundreds of police interviews in the immediate aftermath yielded little, according to newspaper reports. There were a number of leads pursued at the time, but they did not have a clear suspect. They say they do now with the advances in technology, which have allowed authorities to re-evaluate blood-stained evidence, particularly blood patterns at the murder scene, providing a break that police have awaited for decades. According to police, the analyses of forensic experts coupled with statements made to them over the years have officers on the verge of closing one of the oldest unsolved homicides in Western Pennsylvania.

Police still ask for your help with this unsolved murder of Alice Kellar. They have said not to discount the relevance of any information you may know. Your piece of information may have a significant impact on the investigation when viewed in the context of what they already know. For further information, call the Butler County Sheriff's Department at (724) 284-5245, or you can E-mail whokilled@rooftoppublishing.com, and we will pass along this information.

Dominick Peoples

Dominick R. Peoples of Ambridge, Pennsylvania, was twenty-five years old at the time of his death. His body was discovered along Interstate 79 in Jackson on December 1, 1977. Dominick had been missing since November 22, 1977. The cause of death was multiple stab wounds. This is all of the information that could be found at this time.

Police still ask for your help with this unsolved murder of Dominick Peoples. They have said not to discount the relevance of any information you may know. Your piece of information may have a significant impact on the investigation when viewed in the context of what they already know. For further information, call the Pennsylvania State Police at (717) 783-5524, or you can E-mail whokilled@rooftoppublishing.com, and we will pass along this information.

Timothy Saloom

Timothy E. Saloom knew his killer, according to police. No one had heard from the unemployed man for four days, so one of his five brothers went looking for him on February 8, 1991. Saloom, twenty-eight, the son of respected physician Raymond J. Saloom, had been shot once in the head. His body lay on a couch in his home in Harrisville, Butler County, where the victim had lived alone since his mother's recent death. Police have been able to draw some conclusions about the killer based on the way that Saloom's body was positioned. It is felt that the person who did it knew Timothy Saloom based on all the crime-scene dynamics. But officers would not detail those "post-offense behavior" clues.

Police still ask for your help with this unsolved murder of Timothy Saloom. They have said not to discount the relevance of any information you may know. Your piece of information may have a significant impact on the investigation when viewed in the context of what they already know. For further information, call the Butler County Sheriff's Department at (724) 284-5245, or you can E-mail whokilled@rooftoppublishing.com, and we will pass along this information.

Vicki Sinz

Vicki L. Sinz, twenty-two, of Butler was found on July 25, 1981, near Geibel Road and Route 422 in Summit. The cause of death was asphyxia.

Police still ask for your help with this unsolved murder of Vicki L. Sinz. They have said not to discount the relevance of any information you may know. Your piece of information may have a significant impact on the investigation when viewed in the context of what they already know. For further information, call the Butler County Sheriff's Department at (724) 284-5245, or you can E-mail whokilled@rooftoppublishing.com, and we will pass along this information.

Mary Stevenson

Mary J. Stevenson, twenty-five, of Pittsburgh's North Side was found on June 4, 1988, at an abandoned strip mine near Stanford Road and Interstate 79 in Muddy Creek. She had been shot in the head.

Police still ask for your help with this unsolved murder of Mary J. Stevenson. They have said not to discount the relevance of any information you may know. Your piece of information may have a significant impact on the investigation when viewed in the context of what they already know. For further information, call the Pennsylvania State Police at (717) 783-5524, or you can E-mail whokilled@rooftoppublishing.com, and we will pass along this information.

Mary Burke

Mary M. Burke, thirty-one, of Penn Township, was found on September 26, 1979, at her home. The cause of death was strangulation.

Police still ask for your help with this unsolved murder of Mary M. Burke. They have said not to discount the relevance of any information you may know. Your piece of information may have a significant impact on the investigation when viewed in the context of what they already know. For further information, call the Pennsylvania State Police at (717) 783-5524, or you can E-mail whokilled@rooftoppublishing.com, and we will pass along this information.

Emily Johnson

Emily I. Johnson was found murdered by the state police on June 11, 1990. Police found her body on the kitchen floor of her home in rural Clinton Township. She had been shot once in the back of her head. Investigators have little to guide them in the search for a killer. They believe Ms. Johnson was washing dishes at the time. There were no signs of a struggle, authorities said, and the .22-caliber murder weapon has not been found. Ms. Johnson's friends and family members have their own theories about the crime. In an interview with the *Pittsburgh Post* in July of 1991, they voiced their opinions and offered a reward for $25,000 to back it up.

"We want to reach the person who committed this crime and haunt him," said Robert Gary, Ms. Johnson's nephew. "He's out there ... He hasn't forgotten the situation, and we haven't either." Gary, a Bethel Park police officer, said the family believes someone in the community knows what happened to his aunt. "Maybe this person bragged a bit ... told someone about it. The reward may jog someone's memory."

Police still ask for your help with this unsolved murder of Emily Johnson. They have said not to discount the relevance of any information you may know. Your piece of information may have a significant impact on the investigation when viewed in the context of what they already know. For further information, call the Pennsylvania State Police at (717) 783-5524, or you can E-mail whokilled@rooftoppublishing.com, and we will pass along this information.

Research and development for this chapter was made possible by the assistance of the Allegheny County Public Library, the *Pittsburgh Post* and *Tribune-Review* in Greensburg, the Butler County Sheriff's Department, Pennsylvania State Police, city police, and the friends and family of each victim.

Who's Killing Under Protection of The Code?

More and more witnesses to murder have become silenced across the nation, bringing law enforcement to an almost standstill. The reason is the "Gangster Code," or "G-code" in street slang. In layman's terms, this is a code of silence that forbids a person from identifying or testifying against a person—even if that person has witnessed cold-blooded murder. If you break this code, you're subject to being killed yourself. Or worse, your family may be executed while you look on. Until the last ten years or so, a code of this magnitude was only heard of in organized crime such as the Mafia. Things have changed; now this code of silence has found its way to everyday life in cities such as Pittsburgh and surrounding communities. It's like having a license to kill.

Police and the courts have been duped by more and more eyewitnesses coming forward to identify a killer, and within the time it takes them to make an arrest and bring the defendant to court, the witnesses recant or don't remember who or what they actually saw. Within this chapter are unsolved murders for which the police have suspects but aren't able to make the case stick because an eyewitness refuses to identify and/or testify against the suspect.

William Stribling

Pittsburgh Police Lieutenant Kevin Kraus believes dozens of people saw who shot and killed William Stribling in broad daylight on a Hill District street on June 27, 2005. But Striblings' murder remains unsolved because none of the witnesses provided information to police. Law enforcement officials say there is a variety of reasons why witnesses don't come forward. Some adhere to a code of silence, some do not want to be considered a snitch, while others are afraid of retaliation. And, in many neighborhoods, there's a general mistrust of police that keeps people from coming forward.

Dennis Logan, a former city homicide detective, said it takes finesse to question reluctant witnesses and establish trust in the police. He said you should never question someone in front of a crowd. When the police cars pull out and the police tape is taken down, these people still have to live there. Logan said he grew annoyed with a trend he saw in many murder cases. Women were much more likely to come forward out of a sense of moral obligation than men. "The so-called tough guys of the neighborhood would never speak up," he said. "That really bothered me, that it was left to the women to come forward. That needs to stop. Men need to take responsibility for their communities as much as women."

Milton Colbert

Moments before a coroner's hearing into his killing, the man who claimed he knew who shot Colbert stood up and walked out the door. In the morgue's hallway, surrounded by white marble and the faint stink of formaldehyde, the reluctant witness told the prosecutor he feared for his life. He would not testify.

Colbert's mother, Carmen Davis, and her daughters, Aziza Wood and Tisha Colbert, came that morning expecting to see the courts take away the man who allegedly had taken Milton away two months earlier on June 18, 2003. Instead, they watched unbelieving as sheriff's deputies led the accused man, Aaron Bundridge, to freedom. Locked together, mother and daughters walked out behind him, into the crowded cracks of the justice system.

"They just let him go," said Davis. Justice walked out on Milton Colbert. They hear from neither investigators nor witnesses. They ache, they weep, and they hope every day for the dawn of a conviction. They are not alone.

Her son had planned to attend Slippery Rock University of Pennsylvania on a track scholarship in the fall of 2003. He wanted to be a gym teacher, said Davis, a quiet woman whose voice sinks just above a whisper when speaking of her son's last days and the time she spent helping him get ready for the move to college. "He had his dorm room and everything."

What's both alarming and sad is the fact that Milton's family have seen the alleged killer on numerous occasions in town since the hearing and feel helpless to do anything. "I've seen him three times," Davis said of the man police say murdered her son. "I get nauseous every time I see him, and I start praying because I don't want to be on the news."

Rayshawn Felton

Rayshawn Felton was the peacemaker in his family, always the first to quell an argument or smooth over a disagreement, relatives said. His nature makes it that much harder for his sister, Rana Felton, to understand why someone gunned down the seventeen-year-old on a Duquesne street last summer. No one has come forward with information on the homicide, which further frustrates his family. "I know there were dozens of people out on that street, and no one will say what they saw," said Felton, of Duquesne. "What if that was their loved one? Wouldn't they want someone to speak up and help solve the murder?"

The Taylor Allderdice High School senior was walking in the 100 block of North Third Street about 6:30 p.m. on July 25 when someone shot him once in the chest. Neighbors reported hearing gunshots, but most said they didn't look for the source of the gunfire because they were so used to hearing it, Allegheny County detectives said. Duquesne police found Felton dead on the sidewalk in front of a vacant lot. County Police Detective Michael Peairs said investigators haven't determined a motive for the slaying. Felton said her brother was a talented football player. He also enjoyed wrestling and swimming, she said.

"He was an excellent football player," she said. "Playing football was what he wanted to do with his life." Rayshawn Felton's father, Joel Corbett, said his son's goal was to attend college on a football scholarship. "He was outgoing and funny and always joking," said Corbett, of Penn Hills. "Everybody loved him. He wasn't a troublemaker. He wasn't out there running the street, carrying guns, and dealing drugs. He used athletics to keep himself out of trouble. He had good manners and was very respectful to adults." Corbett said he struggles to understand his son's slaying and the fact that the person responsible has yet to be charged. "That person is still walking the streets, and my son is dead and buried," Corbett said.

Ronald Sisco

Ronald Sisco, fifteen, was gunned down in Penn Hills over Memorial Day weekend in 2004 in an apparent mistaken-identity slaying, and Allegheny County detectives are still trying to find his killer. Sisco spent the afternoon of May 30, 2004, visiting with his cousin, also fifteen, at a home on Mt. Carmel Road, said Police Lieutenant Christopher Kearns. The two decided to walk to visit a friend on Grove Road, but halfway there, Sisco decided to return to his cousin's home to get a bicycle. Sisco's cousin continued walking to Grove Road, and Sisco retrieved the bicycle. He was riding along Orlan Place when witnesses said two cars pulled up beside him.

At least one shooter stepped from the cars, described as a black car with a red pinstripe and a small red car, and began firing at Sisco, Kearns said. The cars sped off while witnesses called 911. Sisco was shot several times, and investigators recovered seven 9 mm shell casings, said Detective Michael Peairs. Sisco was pronounced dead at the scene. Kearns said investigators didn't get witness descriptions of the shooter or shooters.

Detectives believe the assailants confused Sisco with someone else. Kearns said investigators received information that a group of teens in Penn Hills was looking for another teen they believed was responsible for robberies and shootings in the neighborhood in the months before Sisco was shot. "The victim was targeted for a retaliation shooting, but we've found no evidence that he was involved in any of the earlier incidents," Kearns said. "It was a case of mistaken identity. This was a young kid and a very bold and brazen act, in daylight, in a quiet residential neighborhood on a holiday weekend. We believe there are people out there who know who these shooters are."

Rasheeda and Jaleel Bell

Rasheeda and Jaleel Bell were brother and sister. On August 13, 2001, Jaleel, pictured to the left, had just stopped by to visit Rasheeda, pictured below, in her new apartment. As her brother arrived, Rasheeda was in a happy and teasing mood that Saturday afternoon when she spoke by phone with her mother. "She was happy. Then she screamed. It was more like a yell than a scream," said Bell's aunt Debbie Rankin of Penn Hills. "We don't know what happened. She screamed. The phone went dead. That's all we know."

At the other end of the line, Bell's mother, Deborah Tarrant of Penn Hills, redialed her daughter's phone number. Over the next several hours, Tarrant would repeatedly call Rasheeda's phone, only to get the answering service. Repeatedly she tried Jaleel's phone, too. She got his voicemail message. For reasons that family members said she can't explain, though, Tarrant didn't call police. But as the minutes turned to hours and with no word from either of her children, Tarrant began to worry that something was wrong. Finally, around 11 p.m., she called Rankin. They headed to Rasheeda's apartment in a three-story house on Duquesne Avenue in Swissvale. Inside, at the top of the stairs, Tarrant found her twenty-two-year-old daughter shot to death.

She ran from the apartment screaming, only to learn from police later that Rasheeda was not the only victim inside. Police found Jaleel, twenty, less than ten feet away, inside the bathroom, lying in the tub. He apparently had been getting ready to shower when he was shot to death. Rasheeda died of gunshot wounds to her extremities and chest. Jaleel died of gunshot wounds to the head, chest, and extremities, according to the Allegheny County coroner's office. Police believe the gun that was used was a .45-caliber semi-automatic. The next day, investigators said two men who were inside Rasheeda Bell's apartment on Saturday may have been the last people to see the Swissvale woman and her brother alive.

Jaleel had been in trouble during the past several years. He was arrested on August 8, 2000, by Pittsburgh police when officers saw him loitering at Lincoln Avenue and Deary Street in East Liberty around 10:30 p.m. When officers called out his nickname, "Lil' Bell," he waved a .40-caliber handgun at them, then ran and forced his way into a home on Deary Street, where he was arrested, according to police. He was charged with firearms violations, aggravated assault, reckless endangerment, resisting arrest, and possession with intent to deliver crack cocaine. Officers confiscated fifteen baggies of the suspected drug.

In November 1999, he was arrested and charged with two counts of drunken driving and related motor vehicle violations. He pled guilty and paid a fine. The previous month, Jaleel was charged with carrying a firearm without a license. He was sentenced to alternative housing.

Harry Coward

Harry Coward, eighteen, an aspiring rap artist getting ready to record his first album, was gunned down at a memorial party for another murder victim. "Some people in that community where I live, they just want to forget it," Lueana

Coward, pictured on the previous page, said of her son's murder. "I can't forget it. I know my son wouldn't forget it if it was me. A woman who was with him as he was dying, struggling to breathe, told me he said, 'Tell my mother I love her.'" Coward was shot and killed on May 11, 2001, during a cookout at a friend's house in Duquesne. He was shot several times at close range by an unidentified person during an argument.

Lueana lost another son to gun violence when seventeen-year-old James Jones was shot and killed in December of 2005.

Taylor Coles

Eight-year-old Taylor Coles was described as smart and sweet, talkative, energetic, enthusiastic, pretty, funny, a leader, popular, a cheerleader, a basketball player, loving and playful, a daughter, a sister, a cousin, and a friend. Taylor was killed along with her father and another man at Mr. Tommy's Sandwich Stop in Homewood on January 25, 2002. Taylor's mother was wounded by the gunfire but survived. Taylor's young brother was also at the restaurant but had left to go to the bathroom as he saw two gunmen donning black ski-masks jump the gate with weapons drawn.

After the hailstorm of bullets stopped, Parrish Freeman lay dying nearby, and Taylor's mother, Terri Coles, grasped her daughter and felt the girl's life slipping away. Terri too was shot in the arm, and Thomas Mitchell, with whom she had been talking, was dead. The daughter, mother, and father were unintended victims, police said, and Mitchell, who was wheelchair bound and unable to defend himself, was the target. As time passed by, city police said they believed fear was preventing some witnesses from telling investigators what they knew about the bold shooting inside a crowded family restaurant. What little bit of information already known was that there were two masked gunmen and one lookout who was waiting outside in a car ready to take off after the gangland-style execution.

Nothing can rip a family apart like the death of a child. And nothing can enrage a community with shock and righteous anger like that very same death. This was a crime so lacking of meaning that its perpetrators must be made to pay. Police knew there were witnesses, and they also knew it would take a witness protection program to entice people to come forward with information. The promise of protection and relocation for individuals who would come forward to identify and then testify against the shooters brought results up to and including the arrest and conviction needed to bring justice to Taylor and her family.

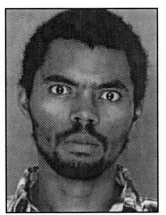

When it was over, an Allegheny County Common Pleas Court jury found one of the gunmen, thirty-one-year-old Andra Crisswalle, pictured to the left, guilty of killing Taylor Coles, her father Parrish Freeman, and his friend Thomas Mitchell in the drug-related ambush. He was sentenced to three life sentences with no hope of parole. The second suspect, thirty-six-year-old William Thompson was also found guilty and sentenced to the same.

When federal witness protection was offered, Crisswalle's girlfriend came forward with her firsthand knowledge of his involvement in the shootings. He had confided in her that he had been one of the shooters. Other people came forward as well and agreed to testify if guaranteed witness protection.

In the last twenty years, 48 percent of Allegheny County's unsolved murders happened in neighborhoods that are home to less than 12 percent of the county's population. They are Western Pennsylvania's most notorious ZIP codes—anchored by the neighborhoods of Homewood, the North Side, and the Hill District, where Milton Colbert died. A world away from courtrooms, most of the 145 unsolved homicides in these communities aren't mysteries. Even police don't list cases like Colbert's as "unsolved." People here know; witnesses just won't testify.

Pittsburgh's witness protection program started in 1995 and has served 500 families, says Sergeant Lavonnie Bickerstaff, who runs the program. Along with police escorts to and from court dates, protected witnesses can receive job training and employment assistance. In some cases, the city will move witnesses to a new neighborhood or another state.

Police still ask for your help with the unsolved murders of William Stribling, Milton Colbert, Rayshawn Felton, Ronald Sisco, Rasheeda Bell, Jaleel Bell, Harry Coward, and Keith Watts. They have said not to discount the relevance of any information you may know. Your piece of information may have a significant impact on the investigation when viewed in the context of what they already know. For further information, call the Pittsburgh police hotline at (412) 255-8477, or you can E-mail whokilled@rooftoppublishing.com, and we will pass along this information.

Research and development for this story was made possible by the assistance of the Pittsburgh Public Library, *Pittsburgh Post* and *Tribune-Review* newspapers, Pittsburgh police, and the friends and family of the victims.

Who Killed the Police Informant?

Informants play a critical role nowadays in assisting police with building cases against known criminals in every aspect of law enforcement. Most cooperating individuals are themselves facing criminal charges and agree to help the police in exchange for their freedom or reduced charges or jail time. Known as "rats" and "snitches" on the streets, they work undercover gaining information and evidence against suspects because the police officers themselves can't. Other informants are "professionals" who work undercover as a way of life and are paid for their services. These individuals volunteer to work for city, state, and federal agencies all over the country. Last you have the everyday citizen and/or witnesses who come forward with information to help stop or solve a crime because they feel compelled to do so.

Most officers do not ever completely trust informants who are only cooperating to save themselves from being arrested or convicted of a crime. And law enforcement does not even like to utilize these people because their motivation is to save themselves, and they will go to almost any length to do so. Credibility can be a problem also, as information they provide is sometimes unreliable or untrue.

Informants have been known to concoct stories and manipulate law enforcement, prosecutors, and the courts into false convictions of innocent people. Some cases are discovered early on and the arrest and prosecution of someone wrongfully convicted corrected. There are cases across the country where years later facts are discovered that vindicate a person wrongfully accused and sentenced to prison for a crime he or she did not commit. Once exculpatory evidence becomes available, it can take years to get in front of a judge, if it does at all.

It seems this is becoming an ongoing problem in our legal system as each week a different news agency across the United States details another wrongfully convicted person being released from prison. More and more cases have involved people wrongfully convicted for murder and sentenced to death—all because someone provided false information and/or testimony during the course of the trial.

In this chapter is a story about one young man who was not only convicted by false information and testimony from an informant, but his arrest and conviction had to do with the death of another informant who was working undercover for police on drug cases against the notorious "Hazelwood Mob" back in the 1990s. This chapter also takes a look at the difference between having money to pay for a lawyer and having court-appointed attorneys who sometimes can't devote the time and energy needed to adequately represent their client. Also included is a look at the day-to-day life of a community ravaged with drugs, murder, and gangland control in a Pittsburgh suburb known as Hazelwood.

Terrell Johnson, pictured to the left, freely admits he was a drug dealer back in the day, but he says he never killed anyone. Testimony by a young crack addict who claims she witnessed him kill a police informant sent Johnson to prison for life. Now it appears new evidence has come to light that shows Terrell is innocent of murder. A Pennsylvania appeals court recently agreed with Johnson and his new attorney and will allow him to present his case in hopes of a new trial. With the help of the Innocence Institute of Point Park University, he may get a chance to prove he is not guilty of murder.

According to the institute, police records, and news accounts, here are the facts of this case.

Terrell has spent the last nine years in prison for killing a police informant. While he says he never belonged to the street gang, he's doing a life term largely on the testimony of a troubled woman who not only tied him to the Hazelwood Mob, but said she watched Johnson and two others gun down the prized police informer. Dolly McBryde's testimony was full of gaping holes throughout the investigation and trial.

While Johnson sits in prison for the rest of his life, the other two men accused in the 1994 gang killings remain free. Harold Cabbagestalk has been charged twice with murder but never convicted, and Dorian Moorefield, whose family has steeped connections to the Hazelwood Mob, was able to prevail over the suspect testimony due to more effective legal representation and was acquitted of murder charges. Cabbagestalk was convicted of conspiracy. But with most of his appeals exhausted, Johnson, who has protested his innocence all along, has little chance of ever going free. "It was an exchange," Johnson said of the eyewitness testimony against him during a media interview at the maximum security State Correctional Institution at Greene. "She saved her life in exchange for mine. Why was this lady's life worth more than mine?"

"Terrell Johnson is a total victim in this case. He should have been found not guilty," said John Elash, who served as penalty phase attorney in Johnson's case and lead attorney for one of the other accused. "Instead, he is doing life in prison based on the lies of a stone crackhead."

"I think it's a situation that a jury made up its mind before it heard the testimony," said James DePasquale, Johnson's court-appointed trial lawyer who admits he was ineffective in representing Johnson. "It was willing to accept square pegs in round holes," he said.

A detailed investigation by the *Pittsburgh Post-Gazette* and the Innocence Institute of Western Pennsylvania not only shows what Johnson is saying may be true, but that the jury of his peers did not hear the whole story during Johnson's trial. For instance:

1. Prosecutors told Johnson's lawyers about some of McBryde's life of crime that included fraud, theft, prostituting her children, and using them to steal. And while defense lawyers were told she was caught shoplifting at a drug store while under Pittsburgh police protection, Johnson's lawyers did not know she was also caught stealing furnishings from a safe-house hotel or that McBryde has used as many as eleven different names and six different Social Security numbers during a life of crime the Johnson jury never heard about. McBryde also received more sentence reductions and case dismissals than prosecutors admitted.

2. From her initial statements to a coroner's inquest to trial, McBryde, who not only had a long-term crack addiction but extremely poor eyesight, changed her testimony on her point of view of the killing. At first, she said she hid in bushes in front of a house to watch the brutal murder. But when she realized her view would have been obstructed from that spot, she changed her testimony to say she hid herself in bushes at the side of the home to watch the killing. Johnson's trial attorney did not cross-examine McBryde on that switch because an investigator did not adequately examine the crime scene, leaving the lawyer to work from prosecutor's photographs that did not show the obstructed view. In the later trials, lawyers took juries to the crime scene and produced testimony from the property's owner who said McBryde could not have been at the second viewpoint.

3. McBryde testified she heard one shot, then another as much as two minutes later after she hid herself in the bushes. She said Robinson did not fall to the ground until after the second shot. Other witnesses said the shots were simultaneous and a forensic expert said either one of them would have put her down immediately.

4. McBryde said she walked to the home of one of the killers to provide massage services in the aftermath of the killing. Her customer, Dorian Moorefield's brother Gary, has airline tickets showing he was in Atlanta the day of Verna Robinson's killing. Two other people say they spent the entire day and night with McBryde. At the time of the murder, they say McBryde was in their Hazelwood home engaging

in prostitution for drugs three blocks away from the scene.

5. A woman and a man never put on the witness stand say Johnson was in their house almost a half-mile away the entire night of the murder.

While the entire case was built on a depraved drug addict's testimony, and Johnson's trial attorney told his jury about Johnson's alibi, he decided not to put the alibi witnesses on the stand because they were of questionable credibility and scared. He later admitted under oath that decision rendered him ineffective.

Verna Robinson, like many young black women in Hazelwood, grew up fast in the late 1980s and early 1990s. The life she knew in Hazelwood was a poor existence of the middle-class neighborhood's decline since the steel mills along the Monongahela River went down. If the closing of the mills ripped at the neighborhood's financial base, another tragedy tore apart its neighborhoods—crack cocaine and the street gang violence that accompanied a need for earning money. Verna Robinson got caught in its grips, and in the year prior to her death, she had hit rock bottom.

She might have used cocaine to endure the pain of devastating tragedy suffered since childhood. Raised by a single mother after her father disappeared, she watched as one of her brothers got sent to prison for twenty years on a robbery conviction. Another brother, Eugene "Butchie" Robinson, died after being shot fourteen times in 1992. Police charged Cabbagestalk with the killing, but later dismissed the case after an eyewitness changed her story and refused to testify against him. It was the second time prosecutors dropped a murder case against

Cabbagestalk due to recanted testimony. Those murders remain unsolved.

While she despised the gangsters over her brother's death, her addiction kept her in constant contact with drug dealers and other criminals associated with them.

The dope life also brought her into regular contact with women like Dolly McBryde, then thirty, another crack cocaine addict whose fortunes would inexorably be tied to her testimony about Robinson's death. Their days were spent concocting schemes, shoplifting, finding ways to prostitute themselves, and just about anything else they could do to raise money for drugs. By the spring of 1994, Robinson had come to a crossroads.

Drugs had ravaged her to the point that Hazelwood residents say she would prostitute herself for a few dollars or less to procure even one small rock of crack. Even drug dealers say she was so consumed with crack that she had no means to maintain her habit. A single mother at that point, she finally decided to make a determined effort to get off drugs. Her mother said Verna was free of dope for two months on the night she died. It was during that time Robinson made a decision that she hoped could keep her away from the dealers while exacting some vengeance for her brother's murder.

At the time, the Hazelwood Mob held a reign of terror over the area. It was common knowledge on the streets that anyone who told police anything about as many as ten unsolved murders and other violent crimes attributed to the street gang would die. Despite that, Verna Robinson told police in November 1993 she watched a drive-by shooting in which Hazelwood Mobster Anthony "Little Anthony" Griffin, a juvenile, was part of a crew who fired a shotgun into the face and back of Eric Godfrey, whose family was in a dispute with the gang. Godfrey survived.

Because police knew of previous cases where witnesses associated with Hazelwood Mob cases had been threatened, Robinson was placed under Pittsburgh police protection for a time. Eventually, she moved back to her mother's home in the heart of Hazelwood Mob turf. Police say she refused their offers of protection. Her mother says her daughter moved home because she didn't have money to pay rent and utilities on an apartment police found for her. Within weeks of her decision to testify against Griffin, Robinson had another encounter—this time with street-level drug dealer Johnson.

She had a long-standing debt of less than $100 to Johnson when he encountered her just off Hazelwood Avenue. She later filed simple assault charges against him, stating he beat her over the delinquent debt. Johnson says she did owe him money, but he maintains she fled as soon as she saw him and fell down the steps. A man with Robinson at the time later signed an affidavit corroborating that, even if a jury would never hear it. Despite that contention, at trial the assault would provide prosecutors with a motive putting Johnson in the Hazelwood Mob and in the killing. Johnson, who never testified, says that is patently wrong.

"I didn't even know she was a witness in the Griffin case. I didn't know nothing about none of this stuff."

Johnson moved with his mother and brother into Hazelwood as a child. By the time he turned eighteen years old, he had dropped out of school and done six months in a juvenile boot camp for drug-related crimes. Then it was back to the streets where he said he sold his dope as a "lone wolf," or unaffiliated with the Hazelwood Mob. He said he knew the gangsters but was not part of it. Local cops say that is nonsense. They say anyone selling drugs in Hazelwood would be franchised by the street gang, or else. Despite Johnson's contentions, shortly after

Dolly McBryde told her story to police, his role grew from an independent street dealer to being part of a team of Hazelwood Mob hit men charged with capital murder.

"They tied me in with these dudes that I prided myself in staying away from," he said.

On the day before she died, Verna Robinson had two court dates, one to face Johnson in a preliminary hearing over her charges of simple assault against him and the other in juvenile court to provide testimony against Griffin in the Godfrey case. She was already at the Allegheny County Courthouse when she found both hearings were postponed.

Two Pittsburgh police detectives gave her a ride to her mother's Almeda Street home, flipping her $20 before dropping the prized witness off in the heart of Hazelwood Mob turf. Her mother said she was outraged when the cops arrived with Verna. "People were dropping like flies around here. I was getting shaky in my own life because there were so many people shooting people," Barbara Robinson said. While police contend her daughter refused protection, she says police told her they had found a safe haven for Verna in East Liberty, but they did not have enough money to cover her rent and utility bills.

"They came to me and said it's going to cost $1,500 a month to take care of my daughter," said Barbara Robinson, who had no money. "I said … 'they are going to kill my child!'" Barbara Robinson said police told her "nothing is going to happen to her."

The steamy night of July 21, 1994, led most folks in Hazelwood outside to sit, talk, drink, and watch their children play until past midnight. Verna Robinson relaxed from her stressful day, drinking beer from a Styrofoam cup poured from a sixteen-ounce can of Stroh's she purchased with some of the money the cops gave her. As the night wore on, she listened to gospel music on a Walkman as she pranced around the streets.

Shortly after 1 a.m., Barbara Robinson heard the first shot. "I was upstairs in the bedroom closing the window when I heard the shot, BANG! Oh my God! Before I could get to the door, I heard another shot. Somebody was banging on my door. 'Ms. Barb, Verna's in the street, she's done been shot.' I came back through the house and went out the front and saw her lying there." Her daughter was dead. The faint sounds of gospel music from Verna's Walkman headset could be heard in the air. Later, McBryde would not only have no recollection of what Robinson was wearing but never mentioned her headphones.

"I couldn't say nothing. I just picked up her hand ... the music was playing, then I went back into the house," Barbara Robinson said.

One area resident offered police descriptions of the assailants. She described them as Dorian Moorefield, a man who resembled Cabbagestalk, and a kid between thirteen and fourteen years old, much smaller with lighter skin than Johnson's dark complexion. Dolly McBryde's name does not appear on any initial police reports. The Robinson murder was big news in Pittsburgh because of her status as a witness. Within days of the murder, Johnson learned his name had appeared as a suspect in a newspaper article due to the assault charge. Johnson went to police and claimed he had witnesses to prove he was in a house several blocks away at the time of the murder. He has never wavered from that claim. Police released him but told him not to leave town.

Two and a half weeks later, Dolly McBryde was caught shoplifting at Century III Mall. She had several outstanding warrants for various theft-related cases and for failing to appear in court. She also faced more than thirty violations of earlier probationary sentences that could have caused a judge to imprison her for many years. During her arrest, she told mall police she had information about the Robinson murder. She wanted a deal.

Pittsburgh police detectives met with her shortly after her arrival at the Allegheny County Jail. The cops say they talked with her but because she was under the influence of drugs, only took a four-paragraph statement before she was sent to the first of two drug rehabilitation programs. She would be tossed out of one of them for trying to procure drugs. A state welfare program paid the initial costs. The Allegheny County district attorney would pick up almost $10,000 of the final tab for rehab, housing, food, and clothing before she testified against Johnson.

On December 27, 1994, more than five months after the killing, McBryde gave police her first full account of Robinson's murder. She said she was hanging around the now-closed Mr. Z's bar at Almeda Street and Second Avenue, just down the hill from the murder scene even though no one has been able to corroborate that. She said she agreed to meet a man named Tony Wright in a nearby second-floor apartment to drink and do drugs. She described the second-floor apartment just three doors down a hill from the murder scene as a sparsely furnished drug den. When she got there, she said, she found Wright on a couch nodding in and out of consciousness from an injection of heroin. Despite her addiction, she said she walked past a pile of heroin on a table because she feared someone was setting her up. Later in court she would not be able to identify Wright.

As she stood in the apartment, Verna Robinson came out of the bathroom. She figured Robinson was there for drugs too even though toxicology reports later showed no trace of drugs in the dead woman's system. They exchanged small talk and

Robinson left, McBryde said. After Robinson left, McBryde said she looked out a window to watch her friend walk up the street. Then she said she left the apartment to pursue her. As she exited the building, McBryde said, she heard a shot. She said she ducked down into bushes in front of a house at the corner of Almeda and Sunnyside streets.

She said she peered up Sunnyside Street after the first shot and saw Dorian Moorefield, Cabbagestalk, and Johnson surrounding a still-standing Robinson. That's when she said Cabbagestalk yelled: "Like your brother, bitch, this is what snitches get." A second shot was fired into Robinson's head and she hit the ground, McBryde said. McBryde also said someone yelled, "Let's roll!" and the trio fled down Almeda Street to a rusted orange Pontiac Trans Am driven by a man she identified as "Andre." There would be no further mention of the getaway car or its driver.

After she watched the assailants escape, McBryde said, she walked three blocks to the home of Gary Moorefield, Dorian Moorefield's brother and a leader of the Hazelwood Mob who is now serving a federal prison sentence. Despite the horror of watching the gangland-style hit, she said Gary Moorefield invited her into the house to give him a massage. A drug expert later testified that in street jargon, the word *massage* means the exchange of sexual favors for drugs. Within minutes, she said several men arrived and summoned Gary Moorefield with the gang's distress call of "Ou! -Ou! -Ou!"

She identified Johnson, Cabbagestalk, and Dorian Moorefield by their voices. When Gary Moorefield told her to leave, she went next door to Gail Robinson's house where they hid to avoid police canvassing the area. After Johnson was convicted, Robinson, another crack addict who is not related to Verna

Robinson, would tell a different story about McBryde's actions that night.

Johnson turned himself in when he learned an arrest warrant was issued. He would never be free again. Cabbagestalk was caught after a foot chase with police in the Terrace Village housing project two days later. He tossed away a 9-millimeter handgun during the pursuit. It was not the gun that killed Verna Robinson. No gun was ever connected to the murder. Moorefield was on the lam for about a year before he turned himself in. Johnson said police told him they knew he wasn't the shooter. They were willing to cut him a deal if he would lay the blame on the other two. "They told me, 'These guys don't care nothing about you; tell us what you know,'" Johnson said. "I told them, 'How am I going to tell you something I don't know?'"

Johnson knew McBryde from the streets, but he had no idea she was the star prosecution witness until a coroner's inquest months later. His reaction: "Honestly, I started laughing. What could she possibly come in and say? I figured I'm going home." But after McBryde's inquest testimony, the case was held for court. "I was in disbelief. This lady was sitting there lying. I didn't know anything about any deal she got. I didn't know why she was doing this," he said. As his trial date approached, Johnson, who was jailed without bond, became increasingly alarmed. The court-appointed counsel's investigator did not seem to be interviewing key witnesses or examining the crime scene. There was no detailed background investigation on McBryde.

What Johnson did not know was that the investigator did not adequately canvass the murder scene and never submitted a report on his work to DePasquale, who says he mistakenly tried to do the work himself at the last minute. He says he failed his client by not asking for a continuance until that work was accomplished. He didn't, he said, because he did not want

Johnson to be tried with his co-defendants. "You don't go to trial without touching all of the bases, and all of them were not touched," he said.

Johnson said he had feelings of being led to slaughter as his trial began and Assistant Allegheny County District Attorney Kim Berkeley-Clark told the jury: "You will learn that sometimes you have to rely on the testimony of people that have criminal records, people that have charges pending, people that are drug addicts. Some of you may not like her and we're not asking you to like her. What we are asking you to do is believe her."

DePasquale countered, stating: "This case should never have been brought ... this is a case of innuendo."

McBryde admitted to retail theft charges, receiving stolen property, and bad check cases in Pittsburgh, Johnstown, and Virginia during three years on crack cocaine. She admitted having pending charges in which she was accused of being paid by a man to watch her preteen children perform sex acts on each other. She also admitted being charged with using her children to shoplift from a Robinson Towne Center store. She testified that in exchange for her testimony, prosecutors dismissed some theft charges and she received drug rehabilitation and money for living expenses. She insisted she was not receiving any preferential treatment in the child prostitution charge or the Robinson Towne Center cases. In fact, Prosecutor Clark wrote a letter to DePasquale prior to trial, saying the district attorney's office had considered helping McBryde with those charges, but said it "would not do so because of the nature of the allegations."

"What, if any promises have been made to you concerning the disposition of your cases to get you to testify?" Berkeley-Clark asked McBryde in front of Johnson's jury.

"None," McBryde replied while stating she hoped more consideration might be forthcoming. She also said she was off drugs, but she had said that to judges before. DePasquale, like other defense attorneys as these cases unfolded, thought more deals were forthcoming, arguing prosecutors were withholding evidence from him. Under criminal law regarding discovery rules, a prosecutor is obligated to find and turn over any evidence that tends to be exculpatory or would shed negative light on witnesses.

Aside from that, DePasquale says he is more disappointed in his own performance than in any case he has ever tried. One reason is that he did nothing about the aura of gang intimidation that filled the courtroom in Johnson's case. The other was a lack of crime scene investigation. There were instances during Johnson's case where Mob members trying to protect Moorefield and Cabbagestalk not only threatened jurors as they were led into the courtroom, but intimidated witnesses with gang signs and threats. One juror was dismissed after he said the threats rendered him unable to reach a fair verdict. At one point, Allegheny County Common Pleas Judge Lawrence O'Toole threatened to jail one gang member if he uttered another word to jurors or cast any nasty glances or gang signs at witnesses.

The intimidation and fear elements were manifested in the testimony of Satera Thomas. In an interview with police after the Robinson murder, she identified Moorefield at the murder scene, another man who resembled Cabbagestalk, and a black child she described as thirteen to fourteen years old whose height, weight, and complexion did not resemble Johnson. Prior to trial, DePasquale put Johnson in a line-up and Thomas could not identify him. DePasquale said when he told her he was putting her on the witness stand to say Johnson wasn't one of the assailants, Thomas told him that Hazelwood Mob members threatened to kill her if she testified. She told him she was not going to repeat her statements to police if he put her under oath, so he did not plan to call her as a witness.

To DePasquale's amazement, Thomas was called as a prosecution witness to show how pervasive the Hazelwood Mob climate of fear was. She showed up in court wearing a wig and sunglasses as a prosecution witness. When DePasquale questioned her about her statements in a police report in the hours after the killing, she denied ever making them. "In that case, things were going wrong, it was just one other big piece of a bad puzzle," DePasquale said.

Elash, who watched the trial because he was appointed to represent Johnson in the penalty phase of the case because prosecutors were seeking a death sentence, blames himself. "I learned at the expense of someone who got life that you have to make sure to control the courtroom. I was negligent in not monitoring the aura of the courtroom ... I became a better attorney over it and he spends his life in prison; that's a travesty of justice," he said.

The jailed Johnson was unaware of most of that, but he knew things were not going well. "There wasn't a time that I thought I was winning," Johnson said.

DePasquale did find some holes in McBryde's testimony. She testified Robinson was still standing between the first and second shot, a fact disputed by a forensic pathologist who said either of the shots would have caused Robinson to be instantaneously immobilized. "Did you or did you not ever see Verna Robinson standing after you heard the first gunshot fired?" DePasquale asked after a contentious series of questions.

"Yes," replied McBryde.

He got McBryde to admit she had been convicted of several felony cases in Pittsburgh, Johnstown, and Virginia.

But DePasquale did not know that McBryde had used as many as eleven different names and six different Social Security numbers during a life of crime the Johnson jury never heard about. Because a private investigator did not adequately canvass the area and the jury was not taken to the scene, DePasquale allowed the jury to rely on photographs taken by the prosecution team that showed a distorted view of the murder scene. He also had no information to attack McBryde's version of what she did in the moments before she saw the murder or on her actual sight lines of the killing. When that information surfaced, it would change the course of the Cabbagestalk and Moorefield trials.

While DePasquale told Johnson's jury that he was going to present an alibi defense for Johnson, he did not call Ruth Roach or her companion, Stanley West, who signed affidavits stating Johnson was in their home six blocks away when the murder happened. Early in the night, they said, he helped them baby-sit six young children. Then they said he went to a third-story bedroom and didn't leave until the next morning. DePasquale decided in a case resting on testimony of a long-time criminal and drug addict, that the two alibi witnesses, who were in fear for their lives, would not be credible so he did not put them on the stand.

He did not call West because he has a criminal record. He says he decided not to use Roach because she was eight-and-a-half months' pregnant and scared from death threats from the Hazelwood Mob and from police. DePasquale said Roach told him police visited her just before the trial intimating they would charge her with perjury if she didn't watch what she said about Johnson. In her subsequent affidavit, Ruth Roach would say: "I feel that because I didn't get the chance to take the stand, the jury never received the chance to hear the fact that Terrell couldn't have been in two places at once."

Johnson saw Roach at the trial. "In my mind, once you put Ruth Roach on the stand, it was over." At the point he said he wasn't putting her on the stand, DePasquale also decided not to present testimony from Fred Rideout, another substance abuser who also later signed an affidavit stating he was with Robinson when she charged Johnson with simple assault, which prosecutors used to build a motive behind Johnson's role in the killing. In his affidavit, Rideout corroborated Johnson's claim that Robinson fell down city steps trying to flee. Because Rideout was also a drug abuser, DePasquale did not consider Rideout a believable witness either.

"I was thinking: 'I'm going to jail,'" Johnson recalls. It only took the jury a few hours to convict Johnson. He described his feelings as "numb" as he waited for the same jury to determine whether he would spend the rest of his life in prison or be condemned to death. A legal argument before the penalty phase of the trial began led to the imposition of a sentence of life without parole.

Cabbagestalk's trial began shortly thereafter. Elash represented him. After McBryde told virtually the same story as she did in Johnson's case, Elash attacked her credibility by pointing out something Johnson's trial counsel did not know. McBryde not only had been convicted of several drug-related crimes under her real name, but she also had a criminal history under several other names, birth dates, and Social Security numbers that dwarfed what Johnson's jury heard.

"Mrs. McBryde, who is Evelyn Crenshaw?" Elash asked.

"Me," responded McBryde.

"Who is Denise Webster?"

"Me."

"Who is Dolly Pearson?"

"Me," she said, as he walked her through eleven names she has used in various crimes.

After McBryde repeated her story about the apartment she visited before the killing, Elash put the apartment's occupant on the stand. Dinah Brown, a nurse's aide studying to become a licensed practical nurse, showed pictures of her well-appointed apartment that contradicted McBryde's descriptions. She showed how potted plants in her front window would have prevented McBryde from looking out of it for Robinson. She contested McBryde's version of the dwelling's layout. She also said that McBryde, whom she'd known most of her life, was never in her apartment. At the time of the killing, she said she was with her boyfriend in bed. She knew she was there that night because both of them were awakened by the commotion after Robinson's murder.

In a subsequent interview, Brown said she was not aware that her apartment was part of the murder case until she was subpoenaed for Cabbagestalk's trial. She said no one from Johnson's defense team visited her. "It is ludicrous that Terrell Johnson is in jail on Evelyn McBryde's word," Brown said later. Elash also showed the Cabbagestalk jury that McBryde changed her point of view of the murder. In her first statement, McBryde said she hid in bushes along Almeda Street. This time she said she concealed herself in bushes at the side of the house. Elash contended she moved her point of view because her first position was obstructed.

Then he asked her how she got behind a locked gate to secret herself in the second spot. When McBryde did not give Elash a clear answer, Clark, the prosecutor, cleared it up: "… How did you get behind the gate?"

"The gate wasn't there. Or if it was there, it wasn't closed," McBryde responded.

Elash then presented testimony from the owner of the house who said the gate had been locked since he lost a key to the lock a decade earlier. While she had identified Moorefield and someone who looked like Cabbagestalk to police at the scene shortly after the murder, Satera Thomas did not reappear.

The result: Cabbagestalk was acquitted of the murder. In an apparent brokered verdict, he was convicted of conspiracy and sentenced to a five-to-ten-year prison term.

"In my twenty-nine years as a lawyer, Dolly McBryde was if not the most incredible witness I ever heard, she is in the pantheon of incredible witnesses," Elash said. DePasquale said that while the Hazelwood Mob held an iron-clad rule over the neighborhood, McBryde said Dorian Moorefield had repeated telephone conversations with McBryde prior to when he turned himself in to face trial a year after the charges were filed.

That never came up in his trial but his attorney continued to pound away at all of the previous issues and argued that McBryde intimated in her testimony that she was given promises of more deals from the government that were not disclosed. That happened as Attorney William Difendorfer questioned McBryde about the charges of prostituting her children and using them to steal from department stores in Robinson Towne Center that caused child welfare officials to take them from her. While McBryde testified she was not expecting any further deals from prosecutors, she steadfastly maintained in front of a jury that her children would soon be returned to her.

That caused Difendorfer, like Elash and DePasquale before him, to question whether prosecutors were withholding information about hidden deals. Difendorfer also questioned McBryde about why she wasn't charged with crimes after being caught shoplifting $7.10 in false fingernails, nail polish, and polish remover from an Eckerd Drug Store in Oakland while she was in the custody of a city police detective.

McBryde also admitted she had severe lifelong eyesight problems. On the night of the murder, she said she was only wearing one contact lens.

As for her story of giving Gary Moorefield a massage shortly after the murder, Moorefield produced airline ticket receipts showing he was in Atlanta. In a subsequent letter from prison, he confirmed that. Moorefield was acquitted in two hours. "Sick," is the word that Johnson said described his feelings on learning about the acquittals of Moorefield and Cabbagestalk. "You're happy that individuals didn't have to go to jail, but at the same time, they were telling me I'm here in prison forever for something I didn't do," he said.

In the aftermath of the two acquittals, Judge Lawrence O'Toole, who presided over all three cases, granted Johnson a new trial after DePasquale admitted at a post-trial hearing that he was ineffective over the failure of the investigator to properly investigate the crime scene and for not putting Johnson's alibi witnesses on the stand. While he admitted his shortcomings, DePasquale testified: "I am as sure that Evelyn McBryde was not present at the homicide scene and did not witness that homicide as I am of anything."

In a recent interview, DePasquale went further: "This is the first case I've ever had where I thought he did deserve a new trial based on my ineffectiveness. The same investigation I should have done was what the police should have done if the investigation was done in good faith. Instead, they started with a conclusion and investigated it until they had a case. In my mind, that's a discovery abuse in and of itself. The reason they didn't want to investigate this fully is that they had enough evidence to build a case. They weren't going to investigate this to find out it was a total fraud," he said. "I don't believe the police or prosecutors believe McBryde was anywhere near the scene that night."

Elash says the presiding judge realized that as the cases progressed. "Judge O'Toole had the advantage of literally seeing the scene and seeing all the additional evidence in the other cases. He gave Terrell Johnson a chance to have a fair trial, which is what any fair-minded jurist should do," said Elash. Prosecutors appealed O'Toole's reversal to the state superior court. In a 2-1 vote, a panel of judges reversed O'Toole's new trial order. Despite DePasquale's admissions, they did not believe his performance merited a new trial.

In a dissent, Superior Court Judge John Musmanno said: "I rely upon the logical and well-reasoned opinion of Judge Lawrence O'Toole ... that counsel's failure to call five witnesses identified by the appellant had no reasonable basis, and thus, that appellant's trial counsel was ineffective. I also note that trial counsel himself agreed, during the Post Conviction Relief Act hearing, that he was ineffective in failing to call at least one of the witnesses."

"The superior court obviously had no knowledge of the record," Elash said.

"I was shocked. I never thought Judge O'Toole would be reversed on that," DePasquale said.

The state supreme court also denied his appeal.

During the trials, Berkeley-Clark, now an Allegheny County Common Pleas judge serving in the Family Division, told defense lawyers once McBryde's testimony was completed there would be no further deals. Not only were the charges that she prostituted her children dropped, but also McBryde has enjoyed other pardons from prosecutors.

"I knew that any charges out there against Dolly McBryde were going to go away," DePasquale said.

Since then, McBryde has been charged with nine additional crimes in Allegheny County. They include being charged with stealing her father's Social Security check on Christmas Day as well as various check thefts, and other frauds are drug-related. At one point, McBryde moved frequently and claimed in some court documents she was in a witness protection program. She had nine outstanding arrest warrants against her in Allegheny County because she failed to appear at court hearings after arrests. In the paperwork associated with these cases, the Allegheny County District Attorney's office left blank various questions on forms that provide sentencing judges with information on previous criminal history.

Under state sentencing guidelines, judges are obliged to calculate previous criminal history, as well as violations of probationary sentences, to increase penalties. If her criminal history was properly documented, under law many of the crimes she was facing would have been graded as felonies. With a long list of violated probationary sentences, she could have been incarcerated for as long as fifty years. Instead, McBryde was given credit for the time she served between being picked up for failing to appear in court and awaiting trial. By the time a series of judges including O'Toole plodded through the new charges, many of them were dismissed and she received a series of probationary sentences to go along with those she previously accepted and violated during her career in crime that now numbers more than fifty cases.

After a long search, McBryde was found and asked about her testimony and the information that had not been brought out about deals in her own cases. She initially did not admit who she was but eventually relented. She showed no remorse for her testimony other than offering a few vague words about Johnson. "He's not the one I wanted," she said. "If he'd had the money or the power like the other two, he'd have gotten off, too. He didn't know what he was getting into; he just got caught up in some bad shit," she said.

Despite her long criminal history, she said she works part-time as a "certified special police officer." During the brief interview, she agreed to talk specifically about the cases later. When contacted, she proclaimed her "time is money," suggesting a reporter pay her for an interview. When that offer was refused, she claimed any published story was going to cause harm to come to her despite the fact that she has been seen in clubs and shopping places frequented by folks from Hazelwood over the past two years.

Terrell Johnson spends his days working in a sewing shop at SCI-Greene and working on his last-ditch appeals. The way he looks at it is that he was tied into a murder case over a simple assault that never happened. He says he embraced Christianity in the county jail while he was awaiting trial. "I'm not a perfect citizen; I was who I was, but look at Evelyn McBryde. This lady took a deal to save her own life ... I just want my life back ... another chance at life," he said.

Who Killed Chief of Police Gregory Adams?

A wall in the Saxonburg Police Department station is dedicated to commemorating Chief Gregory Adams. It contains a memorial plaque along with framed mementos and a photo of the signing of the Bulletproof Vest Partnership Grant Act of 1998, which provides grants to buy bulletproof vests for police officers. Saxonburg Police Chief Adams was fatally shot on December 4, 1980, when he pulled over a car with out-of-state plates in Saxonburg after its driver had run a stop sign.

Chief Adams was not wearing a bulletproof vest when he was shot twice, once in his side and once in his chest. Today, the Saxonburg Police Department holds great respect for former chief Adams. Officer Bergstrom wishes they could have met. "He's a guy that had a lot of experience," he said. "He would've given a lot more years and made the department even better."

The only suspect, Donald Eugene Webb, pictured on the next page in an enhanced photo that shows how he would appear today, has never been found. He is wanted on a federal warrant for interstate flight to avoid prosecution and burglary charges, and remains on the FBI's Most Wanted List of Fugitives to this date. Jim Poydence, a state police investigator who was friends with Chief Adams, was the lead officer in the investigation of his death. He also knew State Trooper Corporal Joseph Pokorny, who was more recently shot to death in a traffic stop on December 12, 2006.

"Both were aggressive, quick thinking, unafraid and exhibited good common sense," he said. "But the circumstances that existed at the time of each of these traffic stops were as unpredictable as thousands made each day by officers throughout the country who simply, by the grace of God, are able to return home safely." Now retired from the state police and working as a private investigator, Mr. Poydence vividly remembers December 4, 1980. He was traveling south from a criminal investigation in northern Butler County when he received a call.

"The initial call came from the Butler barracks, and I immediately knew it had to be Greg," he said. "We were then told the officer was dead on arrival."

Chief Adams' widow was immediately faced with the burden of not only losing her husband, but also trying to tell her son Ben, who was almost three, about his father. "Ben was angry," she said. "And I had to deal with his anger." She also had another son, Greg, who was eight months old at the time. She also had to deal with finding a job and raising her two sons on her own. "You just live from hour to hour and day to day then week to week," she said of getting through the time after her husband's death. "That's just what you do." Adams always found time to spend with his family. He took Ben fishing even before he was old enough to cast a line. "He was a great husband and a great father," explained Mary Ann (Adams) Jones, who has since married.

Mr. Poydence agreed that Chief Adams was a family man as well as a good police officer. "He was a tough type of cop," he said. "He wasn't real big, but he was no-nonsense and always on top of things."

"Not only did his death teach our department in the way we conduct traffic stops, but it helped every policeman in the state of Pennsylvania," said Erik Bergstrom, a Saxonburg police officer.

Officer Bergstrom didn't know Chief Adams, but his death has had an impact on the way he and his fellow officers work. "He made guys more cautious," he said. "You try not to get lackadaisical because out here you don't have immediate backup. It's here, but it might be fifteen minutes away." Mr. Poydence said the job can become routine, but events such as the deaths of two well-trained, experienced officers illustrate how unpredictable it can be. "It brings into reality just how dangerous of a job you have. Even though every day is usually uneventful, you can never let your guard down."

The long arm of the law hasn't reached Donald Eugene Webb yet, but law enforcement officials know it is only a matter of time if the seventy-six-year-old fugitive is still alive. To the frustration of the FBI and other law enforcement agencies that have sought him, Webb has avoided the glare cast by national publicity. In addition to numerous newspaper and magazine articles about the search for Webb, his story has been told three times by the TV show *America's Most Wanted*, and he was featured in an episode of *Unsolved Mysteries*.

At the time of the killing, Webb was wanted for burglary in Colonie, New York, and interstate flight to avoid prosecution.

The car he was driving, a white Mercury Cougar, was found later parked at a Howard Johnson's motel in Warwick, Rhode Island. There was blood on the floor under the steering wheel, leading investigators to believe Webb was shot in the leg during the struggle with Adams.

The main focus of the search for Webb has been in the Boston area, where he has a wife, stepson, and other relatives. In 1990, someone claiming to be Webb sent a letter to the FBI apologizing to Adams' family. But the FBI is unsure whether Webb actually wrote the letter. Such uncertainty has been a frustrating hallmark of the Webb case.

In a 1999 *Pittsburgh Post* article, FBI Special Agent Larry Likar, then head of the Greater Pittsburgh Fugitive Task Force, said that over the years, especially after a spate of publicity, the bureau had received tips about Webb from all over the country. Likar said he remembered getting tips on Webb when he worked in FBI field offices in the Midwest and Puerto Rico. But agents have been unable to corroborate or follow up on any of the tips, he said.

That has led Likar to the belief Webb most likely is dead. As a career criminal, it is unlikely Webb would have changed his ways and not committed any other crimes that could have led to his capture, Likar theorized. Moreover, he said, the amount of publicity given Webb surely should have produced some leads that could be corroborated. "There's been more exposure on this case over a longer period than any other case," he said. "There's been nobody else with this degree of sustained interest without one bit of corroborated information. When the car was recovered, that was it. That was the last link to Donald Eugene Webb."

Nevertheless, Likar said, another theory is that crime figures have helped Webb elude authorities. As a member of a professional burglary ring operating out of Massachusetts, "he had tremendous contacts with the criminal underground, with tons of people who could have helped him. That's one reason the bureau believes he may still be alive. He could have a new ID and never committed another crime. That's a valid theory."

Yet, on the other hand, an argument against that theory is that the criminal element usually doesn't protect colleagues who are hot because that only serves to put heat on them, Likar noted. "That's the problem John Dillinger had when he was a wanted fugitive. He couldn't find anybody to protect him. Organized crime groups don't want a lot of heat. They would have legitimate concern with someone accused of killing a police officer and being sought by the FBI."

Likar said it had been frustrating for agents to get leads about Webb time and again for nearly nineteen years, only to have them fizzle. "The amount of manpower expended on the Webb case has been rather substantial. It's been sporadic, but every time the case is publicized, there's a rash of activity across the country. But that's the way it should be for the murder of a police chief. We should never give up."

Police still ask for your help with this unsolved murder of Chief Gregory Adams. They have said not to discount the relevance of any information you may know about the whereabouts of Donald Eugene Webb or any information concerning Chief Adams' murder. Your piece of information may have a significant impact on the investigation when viewed in the context of what they already know. For further information, call the Pittsburgh FBI at (412) 432-4000, or you can E-mail whokilled@rooftoppublishing.com, and we will pass along this information.

Research and development for this chapter was made possible by the assistance of the Allegheny County Public Library, the *Pittsburgh Post*, the FBI, the Saxonburg City Police, and the friends and family of Chief Adams.

Who Killed Michael and Mary Brincko?

Mary Brincko's brother was shocked to learn his elderly sister and her husband had been murdered, but he still doesn't understand why. William Banish discovered the bodies of Mike Brincko, seventy-three, and his wife Mary, seventy-two, in a pool of blood at the foot of their basement steps about noon on Wednesday, November 7, 1990. In the beginning, William never considered his sister and brother-in-law could have been murdered. He honestly felt they had somehow fallen down the basement stairs and died together. The Brinkos had lived for years in their home located on West Pike Street in Chartiers, which is near Cannonsburg in Washington County.

Then as things progressed and the coroner released their report saying both victims' skulls were fractured, he soon realized it was murder. Ernest L. Abernathy, pathologist and chief deputy coroner, said the couple had similar fractures to the tops of their heads, indicating they were struck with "a hammer or something with a round head," probably between 9:30 and 10 p.m. on the night of November 6. Abernathy said it was possible that Mrs. Brincko fell down the stairs after being struck on the head because there were lacerations on her hand and legs that may have been caused by a fall. But he said there was no indication the couple was involved in a struggle at the time of their deaths, and the house did not appear to have been burglarized as everything was neat and orderly.

Washington County Coroner Farrell Jackson said the fact the rear of their skulls was fractured and the manner in which the bodies were found led investigators to label the deaths suspicious. Authorities were investigating bloodstains in a basement washtub. Banish said his brother-in-law had frequent, heavy nose bleeding because of emphysema and black lung disease from working more than thirty years as a miner at the former Hill Station mine of the Pittsburgh Coal Company.

The blood would drain through his sinuses into his mouth and throat, Banish said. When that happened, the couple went to the basement, and he would spit the blood into a washtub. Banish said his sister accompanied Brincko because he used portable oxygen and the stairs would be "a tremendous exertion."

State police set up road stops on West Pike Street in order to ask some 400 drivers if they heard or saw anything suspicious on the day of the elderly couple's death. Authorities became aware of, and subsequently began asking for help in locating, a white passenger van seen near the home earlier on the day the bodies were found. State police said the van, a Ford Aerostar, was seen near the Brinckos' home in the 2300 block of West Pike Street in Chartiers about 3 a.m. the morning of their murder. Police did not say what evidence they had about the van or its importance.

Neither Banish nor his sister Josephine Brezinski, who were neighbors with the Brinckos for forty years, can understand why anyone would want to kill the couple married for forty-seven years. Ms. Brenzinski told investigators they were both in good spirits the last day she saw them and that Mike was at her house shortly before noon and Mary was there every day about 6 p.m., just to talk. Ms. Brezinski went to the Brincko home the morning of November 7 and became concerned after repeatedly getting no answer at the door.

"It was a death that didn't have to be," Ms. Brezinski said in a 1990 interview with the news. "I just don't know what to think. When you are so close, it's hard to accept," Banish said. "It's not going to be easy any way. If you do know who did it, you'll feel awfully bitter and that won't do any good because Mike and Mary will never come back. But I hope they get them because they could do it again."

As of this date, no arrests have been made.

Police still ask for your help with the unsolved murders of Michael and Mary Brincko. They have said not to discount the relevance of any information you may know about their murder. Your piece of information may have a significant impact on the investigation when viewed in the context of what they already know. For further information, call Washington County Sheriff at (724) 228-6840, or you can E-mail whokilled@rooftoppublishing.com, and we will pass along this information.

Research and development for this chapter was made possible by the assistance of the Washington County Public Library, the *Pittsburgh Post*, the FBI, the Washington County police, and friends and family of the Brinkos.

Who Killed Bonnie Dryfuse and Her Children?

Thirty-six-year-old Thomas Kimbell was standing near the fruit stand in the small farming community of Pulaski on June 15, 1994, with his thumb out trying to catch a ride over to his parents' trailer in the Heritage Hills Mobile Home Estates. He stood there for what seemed like hours. Finally around 2 p.m. it became apparent no one was going to pick him up when he noticed a bicycle parked not far away. Kimbell allegedly decided to provide his own transportation and climbed onto the bike and rode away towards Heritage Hills.

During this same time period one mile away on Ambrosia Road, thirty-four-year-old Bonnie Lou Dryfuse was talking on the phone with Mary Herko when she heard a car pull into the driveway. Telling Herko she needed to hang up, thinking her husband was home, both women said their goodbyes. It was sometime around 3 p.m. when Thomas Dryfuse arrived home from his truck-driving job. As he opened the door to their trailer, he expected to be greeted by daughters Jacqueline, who was seven years old, and her younger sister four-year-old

Heather. When neither child was there, he did not think too much of it since five-year-old Stephanie Herko had spent the night with the girls and they were probably playing close by.

The first thing that caught Thomas Dryfuse's attention when he walked into his Pulaski home that day was the ceiling molding. The molding had come loose and was hanging from the kitchen ceiling. Seconds later, he found his thirty-four-year-old wife, Bonnie, lying dead on the kitchen floor.

He knelt down to touch his wife's bloodied arm. She wasn't moving. Then it dawned on him how he hadn't seen or heard the girls when he came in. Thomas ran to the rear of the trailer, first checking one bedroom and then another. Then he checked the bathroom. There was blood everywhere, and lying right in front of him in a heaped pile were the three dead youngsters.

Thomas Dryfuse would eventually explain in his own words under oath during the murder trial of his family how at one point he thought he saw his daughter's eyelid move. "I reached for her arm and told her to hold on. Help was coming," Dryfuse recalled. But his little girl had been savagely killed.

Bonnie Dryfuse fought feverishly to defend herself before bleeding to death, according to the coroner. Her hand was badly cut from defensive wounds, and a bent kitchen chair indicated she had swung it at her attacker. The killer slashed the girls' throats before stacking their bodies in the mobile home's bathroom.

Five-year-old Stephanie Herko's head was nearly severed from her neck. Each victim was stabbed and slashed repeatedly. Bonnie Dryfuse was stabbed twenty-eight times, Jacqueline fourteen times, Heather sixteen times, and Stephanie six times. As the prosecutor would tell the jury four years later, "In that bathroom were those three girls, dressed in their bathing suits.

And ladies and gentlemen, this is not too harsh a word, perhaps they were slaughtered."

As police began their investigation, they quickly came up with several suspects. Leading the list was Thomas Kimbell, alleged by family and friends to be a hotheaded, cocaine-addicted madman. Witnesses placed him in the vicinity of the Dryfuses' trailer at the time of the murder. Arrested for the theft of the bicycle, authorities thought they had enough to hold him until they could further investigate. A few days later, they had to let him go when the theft charges didn't pan out.

Kimbell was arrested thirty months after the killings, in part because police linked him with the stolen bicycle that day near the scene of the slaying and he was known to carry a large hunting knife on his side. Sitting in jail for over a year while law enforcement built their case raised issues of just how solid the state's evidence was. They had yet to find the murder weapon and conducting a search warrant on his parents' home turned up nothing. At no time were they ever to find any bloody clothes or other trace evidence.

The only thing they had was statements from jailhouse informants of Kimbell allegedly bragging how he had killed all four victims. Motives began to surface that Kimbell was a drug-crazed cocaine addict who killed Bonnie over drugs.

Finally on April 20, 1998, Kimbell's trial began, and the prosecution was going for the death penalty. Most of the witnesses who testified against Kimbell either placed him in the vicinity of the crime and as near as outside Bonnie Dryfuse's home, standing in her driveway. They portrayed Kimbell as a braggart who confessed or revealed details about the murder that investigators say only the killer could have known.

Prosecutors offered the jury no eyewitness testimony to the June 15, 1994, slayings that he described as the slaughter of Bonnie L. Dryfuse, her two children, and her niece. They presented no fingerprints or physical evidence that Kimbell was in the Dryfuse trailer that hot summer afternoon when life ended for the Pulaski woman and the three little girls.

The seven-man, five-woman jury didn't get to see a murder weapon, which officials believe was a single-edged knife. And the only motive was supplied by two former jail acquaintances, one of them a convicted murderer himself. They said Kimbell had told them it was a drug deal gone badly. No other witnesses linked the Dryfuses to drugs. Several witnesses testified that Kimbell often used crack cocaine. William R. Lester testified he had overheard Kimbell telling a cellmate that he committed the murders after losing his temper because he didn't have enough money to buy drugs. Lester was in the Lawrence County Jail at the time on a rape charge.

He said he heard Kimbell recount how he watched the Dryfuse home from a nearby barn, watching for a delivery. Earlier testimony from Mark Fandozzi, who is related to Thomas Dryfuse through a family marriage, showed that Fandozzi stopped at the Dryfuse trailer around 2 p.m., made a phone call, then left. He was most probably the last person to see Bonnie and the girls, who were outside playing in a swimming pool, alive.

When the trial was over and the jury came back from deliberation, they found Kimbell guilty of the murders and sentenced him to death. Four years later, the Supreme Court would reverse his conviction and send his case back to the Lawrence County Court for a new trial, citing the court erred when defense attorneys were not allowed to adequately question prosecution witnesses. In Kimbell's appeal, his attorney brought out crucial facts that raised questions as to the whole case against his client:

- Kimbell was questioned by police in a psychiatric ward of a hospital without Miranda warnings.

- Kimbell was arrested on a theft charge and questioned about a multiple homicide.

- A police officer testified he had once seen the defendant with a small knife at an unspecified time in the past.

- Photographs of blood-covered bodies of children were admitted in spite of an absence of scientific evidence that linked Kimbell to the blood.

- Kimbell's lawyer was not allowed to cross-examine a major witness who had previously testified that another man, the victim's husband, was present at the scene.

- The investigative process was somewhat suspicious.

- There was no forensic evidence of fingerprints or DNA linking Kimbell to the crime.

- Later-day DNA evidence revealed Dryfuse's husband's DNA in the rooms where the children were found murdered.

- Bonnie Dryfuse outweighed Kimbell by more than a hundred pounds and her body had bruises from a struggle. Kimbell had a complete physical examination one day after the crime that revealed no marks or bruises. Kimbell was a known hemophiliac and bruised easily.

At the conclusion of the second trial in 2002, Thomas Kimbell was found not guilty. As the jury foreman read the not guilty verdict on all four murder charges, Kimbell was overheard leaning over to his attorney asking, "What does this mean?"

To this date, there have been no further arrests for the murders of Bonnie Lou Dryfuse, seven-year-old Jacqueline, four-year-old Heather, and five-year-old Stephanie Herko. It has been five years since Thomas Kimbell was found not guilty. Someone knows something that can bring the true murderer to face justice.

Police still ask for your help with the unsolved murders of Bonnie Lou Dryfuse, Jacqueline, Heather, and Stephanie Herko. They have said not to discount the relevance of any information you may know about their murder. Your piece of information may have a significant impact on the investigation when viewed in the context of what they already know. For further information, call the Lawrence County Sheriff's Department at (724) 656-2190, or you can E-mail whokilled@rooftoppublishing.com, and we will pass along this information.

Research and development for this chapter was made possible by the assistance of the Lawrence County Public Library, the *Pittsburgh Post*, the FBI, the Lawrence County police, and friends and family of the victims.

Other Unsolved Murder Cases Throughout Pennsylvania

UNIDENTIFIED HOMICIDE VICTIM

FORENSIC ARTIST'S SKETCH
UNKNOWN BLACK FEMALE
HOMICIDE VICTIM

Unidentified Homicide Victim — (Date of Release: June 26, 2000) The Upper Darby Township Police Department, Delaware County, Pennsylvania, continues their investigation into the death of a yet-unidentified black female.

Peggy Sue Hogue — The Pennsylvania State Police, New Castle, continue their investigation into the 1983 homicide of Peggy Sue Hogue.

Donald Edward Seebold III — The Pennsylvania State Police, Selingsgrove, Snyder County, Pennsylvania, continue their investigation into the July 1997 homicide of Donald Edward Seebold III.

Charlotte Fimiano — The Pennsylvania State Police, Bethelehem, continue their investigation into the homicide of Charlotte Fimiano. Investigators state Fimiano, an agent for Weichert Realtors, failed to return home after showing a home to an unknown client on September 11, 1997.

CARMELO MOLINA
HOMICIDE VICTIM

Carmelo Molina — The Kennett Square Police Department, Chester County, Pennsylvania, continues their investigation into the December 1998 homicide of Carmelo Molina.

HOMICIDE VICTIM
DONALD LEE SHOWMAN II

Donald Lee Showman II — The Pennsylvania State Police, Mercer, continue their investigation into the robbery and homicide of Donald Lee Showman II. At approximately 8:00 a.m. on April 12, 1999, Showman was discovered lying dead outside of his home in Lackawannock Township, Mercer County, Pennsylvania.

HOMICIDE VICTIM
KONSTANTINOS "GUS" BOULIAS

Konstantinos "Gus" Boulias — The West Goshen Township Police Department and the Chester County detectives continue their investigation into the August 27, 1997, homicide of Konstantinos "Gus" Boulias.

Unknown Homicide Victim — On July 11, 1995, at approximately 1:00 p.m., the Pennsylvania State Police, Embreeville, responded to a report of a body being discovered in a wooded area, east of Valley Creek Road, East Caln Township, in Chester County, Pennsylvania.

Carl Devalia — Chester County detectives, West Chester, Pennsylvania, continue their investigation into the homicide of Carl Devalia. On February 2, 1990, the forty-year-old Devalia was reported missing to authorities, after failing to return to his residence in the 300 block of West Lincoln Highway, Coatesville.

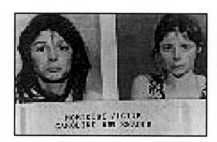

Caroline Ann Brader — The Pennsylvania State Police, Limerick, Montgomery County, are investigating the strangulation death of Caroline Ann Brader. On July 21, 1997, her nude body was found lying along the eastbound berm of the Pennsylvania Turnpike.

Timothy J. Visgatis — Pennsylvania State Police, Hazleton, are seeking the identity of a subject involved in a hit-and-run automobile accident that resulted in the death of fourteen-year-old Timothy John Visgatis on June 9, 1997.

Joline Witt — The Pennsylvania State Police, Montoursville, are investigating the homicide of ten-year-old Joline Witt. On July 27, 1997, Muncy Boro Police Department conducted a missing person investigation.

The Pennsylvania State Police, Hazelton, are investigating the suspicious death of an unidentified white female discovered in Sugarloaf Township, Luzerne County, on December 20, 1994.

Printed in the United States
200087BV00010B/1-156/A